Phil

Where is the Winning Post?

The Biography of
Mikie Heaton-Ellis

HarperCollins*Publishers*

HarperCollins*Publishers*
77–85 Fulham Palace Road, London W6 8JB

First published in Great Britain in 1998
by HarperCollins*Publishers*
1 3 5 7 9 10 8 6 4 2

A catalogue record for this book
is available from the British Library

ISBN 000 274003 6

Printed and bound in Great Britain by
Caledonian International Book Manufacturing Ltd, Glasgow

Contents

Acknowledgements

Many thanks to John Francome for his enthusiastic
support; Judith at Barbury Castle Racing Stables for
putting up with all my calls; Clive, Dean and the rest of
the crew for making me feel so welcome; my editor
James Catford for believing in this story long before
I was able to write it; and not forgetting my daughter
Leah – this one's for you.

1
·······

Praise

There is always a shock in seeing him again. Always a sense of bewilderment in sharing with him his past – even the time between the accident that put him in a wheelchair and the start of the wasting of his body – in memories both verbal and material, stories and photographs.

Physically, Mikie Heaton-Ellis is a shadow of the man he was. He is no longer the sinewy jockey or the assertive horseman or the wheelchair athlete. Medical science says it is impossible for him to reanimate these moments of his existence preserved by a chemical reaction to light and powers of recall that are photographs and memories. These are all that remain, that is why Mikie Heaton-Ellis is only interested in what the future holds for him.

Motor neurone disease affects about five people out of every 100,000 and the onset of symptoms usually occurs between the ages of 30 and 60. It is an incurable condition in which the cell stations and neurons from the brain responsible for moving muscles waste away. Most patients deteriorate progressively and most of them die within three to four years of the first symptoms.

Mikie was a month shy of his fortieth birthday when we completed the final interview for this book in the spring of

1998, approximately eighteen months after first noticing a slight weakness in his left arm. He may not live to see the millennium. This is the harsh reality facing a man whose material presence is fading fast. Because of his strong faith in God, Mikie refuses to dwell or even linger for a moment on the horrifying facts of a damning diagnosis, but they cannot be ignored.

As the disease progresses, both the arms and the legs are likely to become affected by weakness, stiffness and muscular twitching – called fasciculation. Mikie is already paralysed from the waist down, and as the power in his arms and hands diminished during the winter of 1997 he was forced to swap his conventional wheelchair for a battery-powered one. Eventually his grip may weaken to the extent that it becomes difficult for him to hold anything at all between his fingers and thumb, but the most distressing symptom is difficulty with control of speech and with swallowing. The speech eventually becomes unintelligible and even swallowing saliva is impossible. The chest muscles become weak and breathing may be difficult. Worst of all, the sufferer remains mentally alert and there is no impairment in thinking or reasoning whatsoever. They are trapped inside a useless body until they die.

Mikie can feel and see the symptoms of the illness doctors say will eventually kill him and he accepts his own mortality. But something remarkable is happening inside this man; an invisible metamorphosis so inconceivable it defies rational belief. Whether you believe it or not, a supernatural power, greater than anything on this planet, is creating a new spiritual being inside withering flesh and bone. It is as though every ounce of lost strength on the outside is being replaced with supernormal strength on the inside.

On Friday, 17 April 1998 I sat in the living room of the old farmhouse where Mikie lives at Barbury Castle Racing Stables on the edge of the Marlborough Downs and chatted with his father Peter Heaton-Ellis. It is a moment I will never forget because in the eyes of that distinguished old man I saw the three reasons why, against all expectation, there is sunshine in Mikie's life: compassion, humility, and hope.

'It is so terribly unfair what has happened to Mikie,' Peter said, 'but he's made a real fist of things and it could be much worse. There are so many people who are worse off than he is. He has so much going for him and through his suffering he is helping other people cope with their problems. I think it's tremendous that with God's help his life is so full of potential.'

Peter Heaton-Ellis has a theory about his son's illness, and it is not without substance. Medical experts have suggested that motor neurone disease may be the result of a slowly progressive virus infection and Heaton-Ellis senior revealed: 'For years, after his accident, Mikie worked himself into the ground. He really pushed himself to the limit, to the point of exhaustion, and I believe his immune system stopped working properly and failed to protect him from the virus that may be responsible for his illness.'

There is a tendency to look at Mikie and say he's hurt and he's ill, but he doesn't try to hide his condition. He goes out and lets the whole world see it. He certainly doesn't feel sorry for himself and there is no reason for anyone else to feel sorry for him. He loves being Mikie Heaton-Ellis and he truly believes he is doing God's work. Mikie is as happy with each day as anyone I know.

For several years Mikie has been active as a Christian speaker, visiting churches and other groups of people to talk about his faith and how God has helped him cope with problems that could easily have crushed him. 'If it wasn't for God you'd probably be looking at a soggy mess on the floor,' he told me.

Peter Heaton-Ellis does not completely agree. 'Of course Mikie's faith is very important, and I believe that God is very real to him, but I think Mikie is the kind of person who would have coped anyway. He wasn't a committed Christian when he had his accident but he showed tremendous courage and determination to get on with his life. The effect he has on other people, though, must be of God.

'Mikie always got on with people, you know he was the life and soul of the party, but I don't think he was very sensitive or understanding of other people's needs. He was always very ambitious and independent, and still is in many ways, but there is something different about him now. He really cares about other people.

'I'll never forget the night I went with Mikie to a Christians in Sport meeting. A chap introduced himself – quite a famous chap – and said, "Your son saved my life!" I said, "Oh, really. How did he do that?" And he replied, "My life was in a mess and I was contemplating suicide until I met Mikie and he shared his faith with me. He made me realize how much I've got to live for." I was deeply moved.'

It seems inconceivable that someone paralysed from the waist down and suffering from a terminal illness can bubble over with the kind of soul-deep joy that lights up the deepest, darkest places of other people's lives. But it happens, time and time again.

Of course, Mikie is only human and there are times when he feels like caving in under the awful strain. 'The worst thing,' he says, 'is not being able to do something that you've always done.

'Silly little things, like getting in and out of bed or your car. I have to use a hoist to get in and out of bed now and rely on two people to help me in and out of my car. This loss of independence is a psychological hit.

'According to the medical profession I will slowly lose the use of everything and then die. They say it's a downward spiral, but maybe not according to God. That's what I hold on to. His promise that He will not leave me or forsake me.

'Only once or twice since learning that I have motor neurone disease have I felt really down. It's a human reaction but miraculously I have a tremendous sense of peace. It's not a state of mind or a manufactured condition, it's definitely of God.'

Others sense this warm serenity. It is attractive and reassuring. It radiates deep joy. I have spoken to many people who have been touched by God through the testimony of individuals possessing such spiritual peace, although quite often they are surprised to learn that God has used them in such a mighty way.

Once, Mikie met a girl called Sarah who suffered from terrible epilepsy. She was struggling to get through life and agreed to go to church with him. Mikie recalls: 'We went into the church and the normal vicar was away, which was a shame because he was a great speaker, and this old guy was doing the sermon instead. He struggled up to the pulpit, just making it up the steps, and I thought, "Oh no, this doddering old man is not going to do much for Sarah." But he preached the most brilliant sermon. It was called the hot gospel and Sarah really enjoyed it.

'You could really see that she'd been touched by God through the sermon. I was happy for her because she'd been having a real bad time of it. She had bad fits and used to go into a sort of depression for days and just lie in bed. She couldn't hold down a job or drive a car. She was very miserable. I prayed for an opportunity for her to ask me about my faith but when the chance came along I blew it. I was in such a rush to tell her about God that I got it all wrong and didn't make any sense. When I got back home I prayed and said, "God, I'm sorry, I've made a complete mess of a great chance to tell Sarah about how You can help her."

'Eight days later I saw her at Windsor races. I was very surprised because she rarely went to public places in case she had an epileptic fit. It was the end of the evening and she was walking out of the gate. I shouted, "Hey Sarah, what are you doing here? How are you?" She said, "Oh, I've had a great time. I've been with a friend who has been looking after me really well." She was on her own so I asked, "Who's your friend?" And she said, "It's Jesus. What you said made so much sense I decided I want to follow Jesus too. I asked Him to help me and I feel better already."

'Sarah was able to overcome her illness. She still had fits but did not get depressed and was much happier with life in general. The biggest test was that she was able to cope while the epilepsy was still happening. God's strength made all the difference. Sarah prayed for healing and it was discovered she had a blood clot on her brain that was causing the epilepsy and required a very dangerous operation. She rang me up on the morning of the operation and said, "I'm terrified, please pray for me." So I prayed with her on the phone and she said she suddenly felt calm. The operation was a success and now she is working for a charity organization and doing brilliant work. She is also driving and enjoying her life again.'

But things don't always work out that way. Take Mikie's own experience. In between the time of his accident and the time he learned he was suffering from motor neurone disease he went to Hong Kong, where he met the British missionary Jackie Pullinger. She is a remarkable woman who risked her life to share the Gospel message with inhabitants of the vice dens of Hong Kong's notorious Walled City.

Mikie attended one of her Christian meetings, during which she and some of her Chinese helpers prayed for him. During the prayers one of the Chinese helpers gave a prophetic word in a strange language – the Bible calls it speaking in tongues; inspired by the Holy Spirit. Pullinger translated the message which had been directed at Mikie. It said: 'I am the Almighty God. I am the God of healing. Continue to trust entirely in Me and I will complete My work in your lifetime.'

I don't doubt for a moment that Mikie's life is safe in God's hands or that miracles do happen. But one thing is certain: although after hearing such an emphatic statement Mikie never thought for a moment that he would end up with motor neurone disease, it has not dampened his enthusiasm to share his faith with others.

'That message from Jackie really gave me hope,' he says, 'but I never depended on it, never clung to it as though it were some kind of lifeline. I believe God is true to His word and I believe that as I trust in Him, He will complete His work in my lifetime. But it's impossible to predict the future. Only God knows what's in store for each of us.'

A few years ago Mikie received a call from the concerned friend of a man who was suffering from depression and needed help. Mikie was a little scared to share his faith with this person because he was not confident in his own ability to properly explain how God had helped him overcome the problems in his own life. But he ended up visiting the man, who was a valuation expert for Philips, and told him that his Christian faith had made a huge difference in his life and could do the same for him.

The man was clearly impressed and deeply moved. He needed help and realized that the answer to all his problems was God. So he became a Christian and for a while his life was much better. But over the next few years things started going wrong for him again. His depression returned and he ended up taking lithium carbonate to try to ease his symptoms. But he also started drinking heavily which nullified the effect of the drug. He could not cope and shot himself.

'It's a very sad story and I don't know why it happened. It was right for me to share my faith with him but there is not always a happy ending. Only God knows why these things happen. Only God knows the reason for my own suffering. Life isn't fair but God is.

'I feel God wants me to share my experience. When I start to speak in a church or meeting my words come out right and there is this amazing silence. It's not anything I do, but God's Holy Spirit working through me. I can't describe the feeling of experiencing God's presence and seeing people's faces as they are touched by the words God is speaking through me. It has to be the greatest honour to be used by God to make Himself known to other people. But we are only sowing seeds. The rest is up to God.'

Mikie received a letter from one man who said: 'It was wonderful to see so many people in the church to hear you speak and even more wonderful to hear the silence when you were speaking, and one feels only the Holy Spirit could produce such stillness. In the last few days so many people have said how much your talk has helped them to put their own problems in perspective.'

Another letter from a couple said: 'We felt we must write and thank you for your talk. We brought an elderly lady to hear you speak. She has been very ill, suffering two strokes and a broken hip, and sat at the back of the church in a wheelchair. She can't hear very well and we feared she might not hear much. But to our joy we had a letter from her thanking us for taking her. She said: "What a man! I suppose if he had not got such a close relationship with God he might have given up by now. I'd have been screaming, Why me?"'

Mikie: 'In this silence created by the Holy Spirit God speaks to each person. Someone once said to me, "I can't describe how you project yourself because you are not an orator. It must be God speaking through you." God has given me the gift of communication. I know if I went to speak to a group of people about horse racing I'd probably be useless.

'In the Bible the Apostle Paul says: "God's grace is sufficient for me for His power is made perfect in weakness. Therefore I will boast all the more gladly about my weaknesses so that His power may rest on me."

'When I am speaking, I always admit just how weak I really am and how in medical terms, I'm dying. Then God's power rests on me because I'm saying I am weak and God is strong. This is an explanation of why my talks help people, because it's nought per cent Michael Heaton-Ellis and one hundred per cent God. But it's not always been this way and I have felt like screaming: "Why me?"'

Could you blame him? I could not, especially after seeing his past so richly displayed before my eyes in photographs. Pictures of Michael Heaton-Ellis the jockey riding a winner; thrilling the crowds at Earls Court with his horsemanship during the Royal Tournament; flying over a fence on his father's horse at Wyle Horse Trials; walking hand in hand with his first love; standing so tall and proud with his family.

These are powerful images of a life so cruelly shattered and reminders that each one of us is only as fragile or as strong as the faith in our lives: faith as small as a mustard seed that can move a mountain.

2
:::::::

All the Pretty Horses

The morning was dark and cold and without wind. I stood still, a shadow in the half-light, small as a grain of sand beneath the steel-grey firmament and the vast rolling landscape that stretched out before me to the edge of the world. There would be no sun today, only cloud; a dull slurry of cloud as thick as cement smoothed across the sky.

It would not get any lighter than this, and his shape distorted in the mist as I attempted to track his movement across the field in front of me. He was closing but still some distance away. I leaned hard against the iron gate to free it from frozen earth, opening it wide enough to step through into the place where he knew I would wait until our hot breath mingled and flesh touched.

His shape was clearer now, and the morning mist could no longer conceal his striking colour or muscle tone as he moved gracefully and without caution towards me. Only the first time, when we first met, did he arrive with his head down. Now his head was high, eyes radiant, nostrils wide.

We were no longer strangers in the early light and I swear I saw a nod of recognition as I offered my hand to welcome him into my embrace. He towered above me, but bent his powerful neck and rested his head on my shoulder so our eyes were level and I could rub the soft velvet skin on his face, holding his mane with my other hand.

His name is Lucky Boy, but names don't matter when you're here one minute and gone the next. His name belied his fate anyway, so eventually I just called him Boy. Our meeting today would be as short-lived as ever and he wasted no time finding the mints in my coat pocket. He snorted and tugged the material with his teeth before I pulled out the sweet packet and fed him the contents from the open palm of my hand. I stroked his golden chestnut coat as he ate and slapped him firmly with affection when he pulled away. He turned to move off but before he left lowered his head once more and gave me a nudge. 'Until next time,' I said, and watched him until his shape distorted in the mist again and disappeared in the rolling distance.

I closed the gate and headed back to the road. A truck hurtled past, sending leaves swirling over the roof of my parked car, and then the lane was quiet again. 'Better now than a few minutes ago,' I thought. Boy is easily spooked by man-made horsepower and his fear would eventually kill a human being, but I didn't know that then and even now, years after our first meeting, I find it hard to take in.

But it's true, a life ended because Lucky Boy lost control. Yet I would give anything to feel his power pulsating beneath my mortal frame as we ride the wind across the edge of the world and back again. If he fell I would fall too, but it is a risk worth taking – to experience the speed and the thrill of the chase that can make or break a life quicker than thundering hooves cut the fragile earth.

Emma Smith felt the same way before her last ride on Lucky Boy, one summer morning when the ground beneath his flying legs came rearing up from behind a high fence, and together they came crashing down and lay entangled in a broken heap in the great wide-open field of her dreams where she always rode brave and free and immortal.

Emma Smith, 16, broke her neck chasing a dream of becoming a professional rider, and every time I see Lucky Boy I wonder if he remembers the girl with the gentle hands and the sparkling eyes. I believe he does and that is why he has never let another person ride him since Emma died. Her parents retired Lucky Boy the day they lost their precious daughter, but Emma's closest friend, Julie, who looks after Lucky Boy, told me the horse has never been the same since the accident. 'He's friendly enough,' she said, 'until you try to ride him, then he changes. He won't let anyone ride him. It's as though something inside him died the day Emma died. He's lost his desire to race.'

Julie first told me the tragic story of Emma and Lucky Boy a year before I first met Mikie Heaton-Ellis. Ironically the train to Swindon where I planned to meet Mikie in the summer of 1997 passes through the rolling landscape where Lucky Boy spends his life, roaming through that field of broken dreams.

It also passes close to the church where they buried Emma Smith. You can see its spire rising above maple and oak trees that surround the graveyard and the small white headstone with the engraving of a galloping horse. At the funeral Emma's father spoke of his daughter's passion for horse riding and her dream of turning professional, and in a moment of terrible anguish revealed Emma's dying wish: 'If I can't ride again, I don't want to live.'

There were times when Mikie could have been forgiven for wanting to die in the weeks and months following his riding accident, when his mortal frame lay crushed and twisted and broken on a hospital bed.

During my years as a sportswriter I have seen a few lives destroyed and lost as a result of accidents. Speedway riders, racing car drivers, rugby players, the list goes on and on. I have interviewed survivors, some, like Mikie, confined to wheelchairs, others with mental wounds so deep you can see a tormented soul in their haunted eyes. One former rugby player, who had snapped his spine in a training accident, spent most of what was left of his life sitting in a darkened room praying for the end of time and recalling every last detail of his accident over and over again, until one day he wheeled his partially paralysed body to the top of a cliff and pushed himself over the edge.

It is said, and with some truth, that professional sportspeople find it harder to come to terms with permanent disability than most other victims of serious accidents. Maybe the shock to the system of a crippled athlete is greater; the mental anguish more intense and the void harder to fill.

All the pretty horses in the world would not have made Emma smile had she survived to live without her greatest love, and I wondered how Mikie really felt inside, surrounded by constant reminders of what he could have been and what he lost in that moment of madness when his life changed forever.

It was Simon Barnes, a sportswriter for *The Times*, who said: 'Perhaps it is the jump jockeys who are the bravest people in sport.' They face the real possibility of death from their chosen game. That possibility is not as remote as some people within the industry suggest. Richard Davis was the sixth jockey to be killed in action since Joe Banks died of head injuries following a fall in a flat race at Brighton in July 1981. Of the other five, four – Michael Blackmore, Jayne Thompson, Vivian Kennedy and Philip Barnard – died following injuries in hurdle races, and the sixth – Steve Wood – in a flat race.

If you take into account Doug Barrett's death in a National Hunt race in 1976, horse racing has lost eight jockeys in 20 years – an average of one death every two and a half years. It's a sobering reminder of the risks involved and so are the injury statistics.

Jockeys face the total certainty that they will get badly hurt. Sooner or later, and again and again, absolutely no one escapes. A jump jockey can expect to have a fall once every 14 rides – frightening odds when you consider that a top jockey can have as many as 700 rides in one season – and incidents like the one that put Mikie in a wheelchair and killed Davis are repeated almost daily on the racecourses of Great Britain and Northern Ireland.

In 1996 Dr Michael Turner, medical consultant to the Jockey Club, carried out a detailed analysis of the danger of racing – flat and National Hunt – compared with other sports. Turner concluded that in terms of the rate of fatalities, jump racing is four times as dangerous as motor racing, and less dangerous only than climbing, air sports, and riding in point-to-point – a less formal version of steeplechasing staged by local hunts in which all participants are amateurs.

The history of the sport is littered with casualties, both the great and the not so great, whose careers have been brought to an end by injury or the psychological trauma of a fall. While the memory of those killed lives on, those whose lives have been tragically altered by racing injuries are sometimes forgotten. Think of Jonathan Haynes, paralysed from the waist down after being pinned under a dead horse at Southwell in January 1980. Think of Sharron Murgatroyd, wheelchair-bound after breaking her neck at Bangor-on-Dee on the opening day of the 1991–92 season. Or of amateur rider Jessica Charles-Jones, also wheelchair-bound after breaking her back in a fall at Southwell.

John Francome, one of the finest jump jockeys ever, decided that enough was enough at Chepstow in 1985. He was luckier than most. Despite being undisputed champion of the sport, he gave up following an incident that chilled him to the bone.

Francome's last horse was called The Reject. 'It was one of only two occasions I had ever been terrified on a horse,' he said. The other was on a completely wild mount that carried him flat out over fences without any hint of control. But it was The Reject that ended Francome's career. 'I parted company with him at the open ditch in the straight and as I did so he galloped over me. I am not superstitious as a rule but I took this as a hint that it was time to pack up and so that's what I did.'

It was a freakish accident. Francome's leg got entangled with the stirrup leather as he fell and The Reject was set to continue his race with Francome dangling beneath. He wrote in his book *Born Lucky*: 'Geoff Capes wouldn't have been able to prise my fingers off the reins at that point. I knew that if the horse galloped off it would kill me . . . The thought of what would have happened if he jumped a fence did not bear thinking about.'

After being disentangled and helped to his feet, Francome walked far enough away from The Reject that the horse would not walk on him and fell to his knees on the grass. He didn't know whether to laugh or cry and settled for swearing out loud that he'd had enough of riding. This was at the 1985 Cheltenham Festival. The next race was the Champion Hurdle; Francome surrendered his ride. The horse won by 10 lengths but Francome didn't feel the slightest pang of envy. He was just thankful to be in one piece.

Francome didn't give up then but he was never the same. He had another fall – again on The Reject – but this time he picked himself up and decided to quit. He has not ridden a race since. Francome was accused of losing his nerve, but the truth is he quit while he was ahead and it's probably the best decision he ever made. In 1997 I called him to ask if he'd plug this book. 'No problem,' he said, 'Mikie's a great guy, a real character. I'd be happy to.'

I am sure that Francome looks at Mikie and counts his blessings. He has been very lucky and knows it. Another friend of his, Bob Woolley, is paralysed from the neck down after a racing fall.

Francome is Mikie's biggest influence as a jockey. 'He was my hero when I was a young jump jockey learning the ropes. I thought he combined two aspects of being a jockey that are vital. Some have one and some have the other and very few have both. One is being a horseman. Francome could ride exceptionally well. He was in the junior British showjumping team, that's where he learned his horsemanship. He had wonderful hands so that he could guide the horse and encourage it.

'But at the same time he was a good jockey and that means being in the right place at the right time, taking opportunities, judging the pace, having courage, and being prepared to take risks. He was a very good jockey because of this great combination. He just had something about the way he rode. I thought he was brilliant and I always wanted to ride like that.'

'Every jump jockey is one spill away from paralysis,' journalist David Walsh wrote in his article entitled 'Fall Guys' for the December 1997 edition of *Inside Sport*. 'It is the chill of the chase,' he added. 'There is no such thing as a racing certainty.'

It was Walsh who highlighted the plight of Shane Broderick, a remarkably talented young jockey who, at the age of 22, was paralysed after falling on Another Deadly, six fences from home during a handicap race at Fairyhouse. Such was the extent of the spinal damage that Broderick would have died were it not for the work of the Turf Club doctor, Walter Halley, and the team of paramedics at Fairyhouse.

'Broderick's bravery has been remarkable,' Walsh said, 'and when asked how he felt about horses he answered: "If I was all right in the morning, the first thing I would do is get up on a horse."'

The awful truth is that Broderick will never walk again, let alone get up on a horse. But what Walsh did not explain is that Broderick counts himself lucky, compared to Mikie that is. In February 1998, I spoke briefly to Broderick's mother, Mary, who revealed: 'Shane has heard all about the courage, strength and faith of Mikie Heaton-Ellis, and he is encouraged by this remarkable man who is an example to us all.'

Mikie suffered the same fate as Broderick. In 1981 he was paralysed after falling on Dunrose in a steeplechase at Huntingdon. As in the case of Broderick, and other unfortunate jockeys, the fall did not look anything out of the ordinary, but the consequences were horrific.

Mikie's back was broken and he has never walked since. The fact that he bravely put the pieces of his life back together to continue to pursue a career in racing would have been encouragement enough for Broderick. But a few days after Christmas 1997, he, and the rest of horse racing, was deeply shocked to hear of Mikie's terminal illness, the prospect of a slow, painful death from a disease more terrifying for the victim than any fall from a horse.

Someone close to Broderick told me: 'Shane couldn't understand how someone who is paralysed and then contracts some terminal illness manages to keep smiling with a purpose in life. I said, "Mikie Heaton-Ellis has faith in God, that's where his strength comes from." Shane thought for a moment and looked at me. "Can God make that much difference?" he asked. I wasn't sure so I said, "Why don't you ask Him, I guess that's the best place to start."'

Fate? Maybe it was, maybe not. But she crossed my path the day I met Mikie for the first time, less than two hours after the train hurtled past the church where Emma Smith is buried. The Paddington train from Newport, South Wales, was packed on the way to Swindon and I couldn't get a seat, so I stood by a blind girl who had cancer and was going to die. A man in a pin-striped suit offered her a seat but she refused, choosing instead to stand holding the metal rail of a baggage rack and stare into her dark world as we swayed to the rhythm of the journey. She was not pretty and had no smile. Her face was a mass of scars and I was shocked when she suddenly said, 'I was in a car crash.'

She was talking to me and I didn't know what to say. She turned to face me and added, 'I can tell when people are looking at me.'

'Oh,' I said, 'I wasn't, really. Looking at you, I mean . . .' My voice trailed off in an embarrassed stutter. I looked at the floor.

'Don't,' she whispered, 'don't be embarrassed, it's not your fault. I frighten children as well. I know what I must look like.' She laughed and reached out to give my arm a gentle squeeze. 'If it's not too much trouble, you could help me off the train when we reach Swindon.' Her soft Irish voice paused for a moment and then she smiled. 'This is the Swindon train, isn't it?'

We both laughed and I introduced myself. Her name is Mary and she told me a story that I will never forget, not in a million years. Right there, in the clattering noise of a cramped railway carriage on the Wales to London line, I found out why people like Mikie Heaton-Ellis have something to live for, even though in the eyes of the world their lives are not worth living any more.

Mary O'Reilly was destined for great things as a potential champion swimmer until she suffered terrible injuries in a car crash. She was 16, the only child of Teresa O'Reilly, a poor factory worker from Cork. Mary lost her sight and her will to live. Teresa gave up her job to look after Mary and for seven years they lived in poverty trying to come to terms with what had happened.

Teresa O'Reilly was a strong woman and incredibly brave. She had survived the tragic death of her own parents when she was only six years old and the death of her own husband, George, who drowned at sea three months after Mary was born. But something inside her snapped the day she was told Mary had cancer and only months to live. Teresa O'Reilly took her own life seven days before Mary's 24th birthday. She too had lost the will to live.

Mary moved to England to stay with relatives near Swindon. Raised a Catholic, she blamed God for the tragedy in her life but in the summer of 1997, at a Baptist church just outside Swindon, she became a Christian and found true peace with God for the first time since her accident. Two weeks before we met, Mary was dealt another cruel blow when doctors diagnosed her as having Ménière's Disease, a terrible illness that causes partial deafness, tinnitus and vertigo. 'If I stay alive long enough I guess they'll find something else wrong with me,' she said.

'But how can you continue to have faith in God when there is so much suffering in your life?' I asked.

'Because I know He will never forsake me or leave me and one day He will take all my suffering away forever. I have real joy in my heart, angels watching over me, and the promise of eternal life. He has taken away my bitterness and self-pity and made me a better person. God hasn't done this to me, life has, but maybe if I never experienced such suffering I would never have such a close relationship with my maker.'

Mary O'Reilly died peacefully in her sleep in February

1998, but I guess if heaven's got a big blue ocean, she'll be swimming in it.

I sat in the Café Rouge and watched Mikie wheel himself out of the door and into the busy street. Bath was bathed in sunlight but Mikie had a cloud over him; he was troubled. First impressions endure and I will always remember our first meeting. He picked me up from Swindon station and we drove to Bath in a car specially adapted to hand controls. Mikie had an appointment with a doctor at a hospital in Bath. He told me that for several months he had been experiencing problems with his arms; they were becoming weak and he was finding it increasingly difficult to get in and out of his wheel-chair. 'Doctors think it could be related to my riding accident, some kind of nerve damage,' he told me. 'But they are not really sure.'

I looked at Mikie's arms and his hands resting on the steering wheel. He used to be good at what he did; great hands with the sweetest touch and hold of the reins. Mikie could make horses go and when he could no longer do that, Mikie could race marathons powering his wheelchair with these same arms that were now showing signs of becoming as use-less as his legs. 'It must be a big worry for you,' I said and thought of Mary O'Reilly, and how she went blind and lost her looks and then got cancer and Ménière's Disease.

'Yes, it is,' Mikie replied. 'Because I'd be pretty useless if I lost the use of my arms as well.' He smiled and I knew what was coming next. I could sense the same faith, hope and strength that radiated from the blind girl I had helped from the train only hours earlier. 'I know that whatever happens God won't let me down,' he added, and I noticed Mikie's face had changed. He was shining, really shining. I think the glory and love of God came right down from heaven and covered

Mikie when he said that, right there in the front seat of his car on the way to see a doctor who suspected something terrible was happening to this remarkably courageous man.

On Monday 8 September 1997 his condition was officially diagnosed as motor neurone disease. Nothing could have prepared me for what was about to happen but I guess God was preparing Mikie, even though he didn't know it himself.

'Hard and uncomplaining, jump jockeys take the knocks and the falls and still their love for the sport is undiminished,' Walsh added in his article about Broderick. 'Such passion is unusual in professional sport, but maybe what is most admirable is their complete lack of pretension. No jump jockey considers himself a star. Still you wonder why they do it.'

Mikie is tough and uncomplaining and is the least pretentious person I have ever met. Horses were his first love and had it not been for his tragic accident, he may have been a champion who rode the very best horses.

Fate has been terribly cruel to Mikie Heaton-Ellis, and yet one can't help wondering if this remarkable man is actually, and ironically, blessed enough to survive and bounce back from an awful illness that has a 100 per cent kill-rate. Mikie, however, is planning for the future. 'If you want to back a real winner,' he says, 'put your money on God.'

Mikie's illness happened gradually, unlike his accident. That was immediate horror, instant termination of half the man he was before the start of his last race as a jockey. His father, Peter Heaton-Ellis, recalls: 'He was a hell of a mess. His face was grotesquely swollen; one eye was fixed straight ahead and he couldn't see out of the other. He had a broken bone in his neck and his spine had snapped, and it was discovered he had a broken bone in his pelvis as well.

'When he eventually regained consciousness he was getting headaches so bad he used to hold on to the side of the bed sweating. He had suffered very bad concussion and what we didn't realize is that the doctors expected him to be a cabbage for the rest of his life. They were very surprised when he came around and started talking and moving his arms. They also said that his eyesight would be permanently damaged, and that he may even be blind. His injuries were quite horrific really.'

How can I explain in words how it must have felt for Mikie to wake up in a hospital bed knowing he was paralysed from the waist down? I doubt I can, and even he struggles to describe it.

How many of you have experienced the awful panic of sleep paralysis, when your mind wakes to find the body still sleeping? It's a split-second nightmare, like dragging yourself from the jaws of death, and for a moment during the frantic struggle to wake up you become paralysed and fear you may never free yourself. Intensify this terrible experience of drowning beneath the surface of heavy semi-sleep a thousand times and make it last and last and last.

Then, and only maybe, can I explain how it feels when the body ceases to obey instructions from the brain. That very first night when his worst nightmare became reality, Mikie Heaton-Ellis tried to move his legs but they didn't work. Every ounce of mental strength squeezed from his mind screamed out, Move, move, move, but the spark of life was gone and the limbs that only hours earlier had squeezed the pulsating muscles of a racehorse lay still and strangely flaccid on the white hospital sheets.

Motor neurone disease crept up on Mikie. It didn't hit him with the sudden force of the sledgehammer blow that snapped his spine and disconnected nerves like a furious fist tearing wires from a socket. This time fate slid in through the back door of Mikie's life, an invisible, destructive nonentity as silent as a shadow but more deadly than the most venomous snake. It struck without warning but maybe lay in wait for a long time; ticking, ticking, ticking like a time-bomb – only you can't hear or feel the explosion. This disease is a machine-gun with a silencer and the bullets leave no trace; they just kill you inside, little by little, until one day there's nothing left to destroy.

Mikie could be forgiven for being very afraid of motor neurone disease because it will kill him slowly and painfully, unless God, in His grace and mercy, decides otherwise.

On 10 December 1997, almost six months after our first meeting, Mikie and I ate lunch at the old wooden table in the kitchen of the farmhouse where he has lived since 1991 and chatted about his plans for a future clouded by this terrible illness. We had become quite close and I sensed real anguish when he revealed: 'I am fearful about death.'

His words just hung there, for a moment, in the half-light of that cosy, lived-in kitchen with the faces of horses staring at us from pictures on the walls. A thousand memories of less dangerous times whispered of a past so freely given and a future held to ransom by the heavy currency of terminal illness and death.

And yet, from this brave admission of fear Mikie's spirit seemed to rise on silent wings of freedom, his face lit up with all the halo-brightness of faith and hope in the promise of eternal life that he believes God will keep for all time. 'If it wasn't for Him,' and his eyes shone as he looked up, 'I think I'd go crazy. God has taken away that fear of death – it seems to have just vanished.

'I believe what the Bible says about eternal life for those who have faith in God, but when you are confronted with the real possibility of dying it's a different kettle of fish. The medical profession give me little hope. The only thing they aren't sure about is when I will die. Motor neurone disease is unpredictable in that some sufferers live longer than others, but the end result is always the same. Death.

'It's happened gradually, which has lessened the blow. The first time I noticed the weakness in my left arm was January 1997. Within a year it got worse and worse, but doctors thought it was related to my damaged spine. I believed them because it seemed so likely, but tests proved nothing and in the end the doctors admitted that they did not know what it was, although they were not too worried about it. By the middle of the year, however, I was warned about the possibility that it could be MND, and a definite diagnosis followed.

'All the time I have been very well supported by the prayers of Christian friends who have been directed to verses of scripture saying God is in control of the situation. Spiritually, God has been hauling me through. 1997 was a long year, at times it felt like I was in some kind of limbo waiting to hear my fate. The problem is that you can't test someone for motor neurone disease, it's not that straightforward. It's more of a process of elimination where doctors cross out all the other possible causes of symptoms before diagnosing motor neurone disease.'

Mikie went to see one of the top doctors in the country. He is Professor Leigh, a London specialist who deals with motor neurone disease cases all the time. Leigh immediately recognized the symptoms, for which there can be no other cause. Mikie had more tests, but they could not find anything connecting the muscle spasms and weakness in his arms to the spinal injuries he suffered during his horse-riding accident.

'Professor Leigh was 99 per cent certain I was suffering from MND, for which there is no known cure. Some people live six or seven years, others deteriorate more quickly. He told me, "Age is on your side and men don't normally get it as bad as women." It was some consolation but the harsh truth is that I don't know how long I've got.

'I asked God to heal the injuries to my back – it didn't happen. I've seen other people healed but for some reason my prayers have not been answered. I don't know why because I really believe He can heal me. I now feel it is more likely that God would heal my illness than what happened to my back because obviously this is life-threatening.

'I know He can, it's a question of whether He will, but whatever happens I know He won't let me down. Statistics give me a zero chance of recovery but my hope is in God.'

Ironically, motor neurone disease has brought Mikie closer to God and made him more dependent on his faith. Everything else is falling away. He admits: 'I have been very proud of the fact that ever since my riding accident I have always been self-sufficient. I train horses, I go to races, I've competed in marathons, travelled round the world, and even enjoyed going to dances where I used to spin my wheelchair around on its back wheels.

'I know I've impressed people and I've especially enjoyed impressing the opposite sex. I've been a bit of a hero really, but all of that pride is gone. The only thing left is my faith.

'It's not a punishment from God for being proud, or flirting with beautiful women and enjoying the glamour and money horse racing has to offer. That is not the way God works, but motor neurone disease has taken away my ability to be proud. It has taken away the things that I was proud of. The only thing left in my life is the grace of God and He says that is sufficient for me.

'I firmly believe that it is when we are weak that we are strongest in God. Our mortal strength is limited but God's strength is not. If we surrender our strength and allow God's strength to take its place our faith increases and we become stronger.

'Maybe had I not suffered the way I have I would not have come to depend on God the way I do now. I am no longer master of my own destiny. God is, but that's the way it should be, and it excites me to think that God's power is so great and He loves me so much that all things are going to work out for good. That's not blind faith but a promise that can't be broken.'

3

. . . .

Forward March

Michael Heaton-Ellis had a lifetime dream of training race-horses. It was all he ever wanted, and the seeds of his desire were sown a long time ago when he was a young boy. You could say it was his destiny, this nurturing and harnessing of raw and explosive and sublime power that would ultimately turn against him and shatter his life.

It is one of life's great ironies that the things we desire the most and believe will make our lives complete often hurt us in ways we could never imagine. The great double irony of this story is that Mikie may never have had the opportunity to make his dream come true had it not been for his near-fatal accident in 1981.

He was a young, gifted army officer then; 23 years old with 11 winners to his name under National Hunt rules and point-to-point. Great potential, great hands and great future, and utterly undeserving of the awful fate awaiting him. Nothing on earth could have prepared him for what was about to happen as he enjoyed a ride on Dunrose, a novice steeplechaser, in a race at Huntingdon.

The track, near Cambridge, is not blessed with popularity. Former champion jockey Peter Scudamore once admitted: 'I don't like the way the fences are made at Huntingdon –

they are far too black and don't have any gorse in them. Quite simply, horses could be excused for finding them very uninviting. And there is a rogue fence there, the second last, which traps so many because it is situated at the start of the home straight, just off the bend. So that the horses, travelling flat out if they are involved in a finish, and quite likely tiring, have to jump it off balance.'

It was the same rogue fence that stopped Dunrose, but Mikie could quite easily have been anywhere except Huntingdon on that overcast afternoon of 24 October. He had been offered three different horses to ride the same day at another course. At just after 3pm, however, Mikie sat on Dunrose waiting for the start of a race that he would not finish.

He was in fourth place towards the end of the first time round, on the rails and going well, when disaster struck. As they approached the second last on the first circuit another horse swerved in front of them, causing Dunrose to get too close and blocking Mikie's view. Horse and rider crashed through the top of the fence. 'The horse in front jinked,' he recalled, 'and my horse never took off and turned a somersault. I went down and the horse behind put his foot straight on my back.'

Three-quarters of a ton shattered his spine and, it seemed, his dream of training racehorses as well. Another irony was that Mikie had 'stopped' Dunrose in its previous race so that it would still be a novice at the start of the 1981/82 season. 'Stopping' horses – deliberately riding them so that they will not win – though officially frowned upon, is not uncommon. The idea is not to win a race at the end of the season so that the horse is still a novice for the whole of the next season, creating more winning opportunities.

If Dunrose had won at the end of the 1980 season he would not have been eligible for novice races in 1981. The real irony in this case is that although people normally 'stop' horses for gambling purposes or to drop the horse in the ratings to win a handicap, neither are applicable to novice races that are not handicaps.

Maybe, in a different life, horse and rider would have galloped across the Huntingdon winning post and gone on to win other races, but in the end they paid a high price for chasing success. Dunrose is now dead and Mikie stuck in a wheelchair and dying. And yet, remarkably, he has no regrets and never looks back. Always straight ahead into a wonderful future mapped out by a God who really cares about the lives of those He created.

There's a Pete Townshend song that goes: 'I'm looking back and I can't see the past, any more so hazy. And I'm on a track and I'm travelling so fast, oh for sure I'm crazy.' Michael Heaton-Ellis is not crazy. He is the sanest person I have ever met but he is very zealous for the things of God, and I believe that is why he has accomplished more in a wonderfully rich and colourful life since his accident than most ever dream of.

There is no doubt at all that faith in God has sustained Mikie through the years and continues to do so when he has been written off as a lost cause. It's not that Mikie doesn't want to remember what happened to him on the afternoon of 24 October 1981; the truth is he can't because his heart, mind, spirit and soul have undergone major spiritual surgery since then.

'I am a completely different person, in many different ways,' he told me in October 1997, almost 16 years to the day since his accident. 'God has healed me emotionally and mentally, and spiritually I am a new creature. Apart from my physical disability and illness I am complete in God. He has renewed me and continues to do so every day. I don't dwell in the past because of the new future I have.'

Of course Mikie remembers details of his ride on Dunrose, and he has fond memories of the years before and after Huntingdon, but unlike other people I know who have suffered similar accidents while competing in their chosen sports or in everyday life, he has never dissected the facts, or examined the evidence, or deliberated over what might have been had he done things differently or been in another place at another time.

He said: 'I never analysed the accident. I just felt that it was something that had happened and closed the door on it. It is not denial or anything like that, I never thought it was worth looking at, that's all. I just thought, "It's happened to me and that's it, better get on with the rest of my life." You don't want to think "What if . . ." and "Why me?", although of course I had my down moments when it was really hard to cope with what had happened. I had a faith in God then because I was brought up in a God-fearing home, but I was not a believer and had nothing else to rely on other than my own strength of mind, although I believe God was with me. He carried me through because of other people's prayers, even though I didn't realize it at the time.'

I remember interviewing a speedway rider who suffered terrible injuries when he crashed his motorbike during a race, and he revealed to me that he had watched the video of the accident over 100 times in the two years since it happened. 'That works out at roughly once a week,' I said. 'Yeah, that sounds about right,' he replied.

'But why?' He thought for a moment, searching for an honest answer to my question. 'I guess it's because I've never got over it.'

A few years ago I received a phone call from a former top sportsperson who was seriously paralysed competing in their chosen sport. The person, who wishes to remain anonymous, was desperate to trace a video recording of their accident and wondered if I could help. 'When did it happen?' I asked. 'Six years ago, and I've spent the last four years searching for the person who taped it,' they replied. 'I won't rest until I see the video.'

With the help of a few contacts, we got hold of a copy of the video but it did no good. The injured sportsperson became depressed after playing the tape a dozen times or more and began to wish they hadn't bothered.

Mikie never did. It never even crossed his mind until I mentioned it 17 years later. 'I don't know if it was videoed or not. It probably is somewhere but I haven't seen it. If someone said to me, "I've got it," I would watch it, but I don't go looking for it. I don't even know the name of the horse that fell on me, or the jockey. We still don't know exactly what happened, the sequence of events and all that, and we probably never will, but it really doesn't matter to me. Never did and never will.'

One of Mikie's friends quit riding after it happened. 'He said that was the last straw,' Mikie said, referring to his former army buddy Charles Moor, who is now clerk of Nottingham racecourse. 'I think quite a few people were shocked and maybe one's natural reaction is to distance yourself from the thing that causes pain and suffering, but the only thing on my mind was to put the pieces of my life back together and get back into horse racing and fulfil my ambition to train horses. I was determined to carry on; determined to go the distance and realize my dream even though it seemed impossible.'

Perhaps Michael Heaton-Ellis was born with this never-say-die attitude, this driving optimism. As a young boy who spent most of his adolescence either at boarding school or learning horsemanship from his father, a high-ranking army officer,

Mikie earned a reputation as someone who never gave less than 100 per cent. He was not perfect, not always a winner, and he had weaknesses and bad character traits that developed and took root in his life as he began to put childish ways behind him and became a man; a man with an often obsessive weakness for the opposite sex – his Achilles heel – and a quite ruthless and selfish streak. But more of that later.

One thing he is not is a quitter. Never has been and never will be, although now as he faces the greatest challenge of his life, Mikie's unyielding spirit is sustained by faith in God and not the diehard heart that beat out a strong life rhythm through good times and bad until he gave it to God.

There is a wonderful story about Mikie's first winner as a jockey and it illustrates perfectly the type of person he is. He was approaching his 18th birthday when he was offered a ride on a brave horse named Tintagel who had very bad legs. It was 1976: Tintagel, despite suffering from recurring injury problems, was considered a good horse on the flat and Lester Piggott had won some very good races on him.

As a jumper, however, Tintagel could not be trusted and the odds were stacked against Mikie bringing him home with any amount of success. But Mikie was determined to go through with it, even though he lacked race experience and was about to put his faith in a horse that had a history of going through fences instead of over them. Remarkably, they won, and even Lester Piggott, who had described Tintagel as 'a difficult ride', reportedly acknowledged the performance of the young jockey who skipped school to ride home his first winner. It was a combination of faith, guts and raw potential, and Mikie will never forget it.

'I suppose you always remember your first winner and it was a great moment for me,' he said. 'I was still at boarding school, so it made it quite difficult to ride in a race, but I managed it somehow. Tintagel was a real trier but he had very bad legs and he only ran three times for me. The first time I rode him we had a crashing fall, the second time I just quietly jumped him round and we finished third. His legs were going coming into the last fence in the race that he won. He broke down with a damaged tendon, but he was fine after resting and it was a good moment for me. I always tell people, tongue in cheek, that Tintagel had the best of jockeys, Lester Piggott and myself, but he was a great old horse if you knew how to get the best out of him.'

Mikie also recalls with fondness and pride the day he rode a winner on a horse called Quimilt at Nottingham three years later. It was his first win on a proper race track as opposed to a point-to-point, and it was just before his final exams at university. Again Mikie felt the need to put his love of horse racing before his education, despite being warned by his tutor about the dangers of taking time out from crucial studying to ride races. 'I had a lot of work to do before my finals,' he recalls, 'and my tutor had told me I should concentrate because I did all my work at the last minute and had a lot of work to do before the exam, and he said I shouldn't really be off riding.

'The day after the race at Nottingham when I went to have a tutorial, my tutor said, "I thought I told you not to ride horses, but well done." I thought I'd got away with it but he'd seen the result in a newspaper. It was a really good race, and it was very exciting over the last few fences because there was me and another horse going flat out over these two fences and we were both going quite well. It was my first experience of a real race and jumping fences at speed can actually be really great.

'I got the better of the other horse over the last and went away to try and win, but halfway up the run-in my horse started to ease up because it was in front and the other horse came back at me. I had to really push him on but he still won quite well and it is a great memory, especially finding out that my tutor had checked the paper to see how I had done. Just hearing him say "Well done" meant a great deal to me, but I was fortunate to have people like that around me who were supportive of my ambition to pursue a career in horse racing. My parents were perhaps even more delighted than I was, but they have always been right behind me, a tower of strength really.'

Mikie enjoyed and thanks God for a secure, happy and privileged childhood. His biggest influence while growing up was his father, who not only encouraged his son to wholeheartedly pursue his dream, but also played an active role in helping it become reality despite a demanding military career. Peter Heaton-Ellis was highly respected in the Army and earmarked as high-ranking material, but the job was always tough and more often than not required sacrifice above and beyond the call of duty. Mikie, the oldest of three children, was born in Hanover, Germany, on 22 May 1958, miles and miles away from the green and pleasant England where he would eventually earn a living working with the fine creatures that were an important part of his father's life.

Peter Heaton-Ellis, who rode in one-day events and hunted the Royal Artillery hounds, showed talent as a horseman. His own father rode and his grandfather on his mother's side was also a fine horseman. The father of Mikie's mother Pru played polo for the Navy and rode races.

Mikie inherited this natural ability, as well as his father's handsome features and desire to serve Queen and country. Horses became the focus of his life from the moment his memory clicked into action and soldiering was also in his blood, although it was not his destiny to pursue the same long-term army career that served his father so well. Peter

Heaton-Ellis reached the rank of lieutenant-colonel, before retiring to eventually run an antiques business.

'At the time of his accident he was booked to go to the King's Troop, but it wasn't meant to be and it was never my ambition to see him follow me into the army. As a career it was changing and I felt that maybe he would not get the same opportunities I had, but I always felt he may pursue a career in horse racing.

'He and his sister Charlotte would go nowhere without broomsticks because they were their horses. They used to set up showjumping courses in the back garden of the house we had in London. Mikie used to say, "And into the ring comes Charlotte Heaton-Ellis, but unfortunately she has been eliminated. Into the ring now comes Mikie Heaton-Ellis and it's a clear round."

'It was frightfully funny but it was Mikie's competitive nature coming out even at that early age. He was always hell bent on racing. During the school holidays, he used to stay in a caravan so that he could ride out for the local trainer. He kept his eye on all the horses, even at that tender age. He'd come home and say, "Dad, do you think so and so ought to have been out on the gallops today?" And I'd say, "No, you are quite right, Mikie."

'He had a feel for training and he turned into a very fine young jockey. He eventually got a B licence, which means that you've had enough winners to ride with the professionals. He was much admired by the professional jockeys, because of his ability as a horseman and his courage.

'Dunrose, the horse which he eventually piled up on, was ridden for the first time by a well-known professional who pulled him up after three fences and said, "This horse is too dangerous to race." We didn't know this and the following week Mikie rode him and brought him into third place.'

Like many army families, the Heaton-Ellises were always on the move, so Michael was sent to boarding school at the age of eight. His memories are happy ones, although he has no memories of Germany. 'Although I was born in Hanover, I was christened in England and I have no real emotional or spiritual links with Germany,' he said. 'The first place I remember was in London where my father was Commanding Officer of the King's Troop in St John's Wood.

'Then we went to the Midlands, to Nuneaton in Warwickshire, where my father was Commanding Officer of the Junior Leaders Regiment Royal Artillery. At that time I started going to boarding school. A lot of my growing up took place at boarding school, but I did not lose out. I think boarding school actually made me more appreciative of home life. I looked forward to going home and I got more out of my home life than perhaps other children did who were at home all the time.

'I went to a school near Hemel Hempstead called Lockers Park and the reason I went to boarding school there was because my father thought he might be suddenly posted abroad. So he wanted me to go to a school near to London so that he could then fly back in to see me, and also some of my cousins went to that particular school so they knew I would not be completely on my own. Then he got posted to Warminster and I grew up a bit more. Boarding school was a big part of growing up because I always spent so much time there and not so much time at home. And then we went to Larkhill.'

Mikie was given his first pony, Beaumont, when he was seven, before boarding school in Hemel Hempstead, and competed like many youngsters in local gymkhanas during the school holidays. The talk in the Heaton-Ellis household was often of horses. Mikie's brother David has become a professional polo player, but in the early days it was hunting and eventing that took priority. Racing would not figure in Mikie's life until his late teenage years and he recalls: 'I always liked jumping more than the gymkhana and races. My father had always ridden a lot, but eventing not racing, apart from point-to-point occasionally, but that wasn't his game really. He could turn his hand to most things though, he was quite versatile and always gave a hundred per cent.'

Like father, like son. Mikie was also known for his versatility, not just as a young horseman but as a useful all-round sportsman as well. Much later, following his accident, he would return to competitive sport as a wheelchair athlete, satisfying the intense combative hunger that made him so popular with selectors at prep school and later at public school at Radley, just outside Oxford.

He captained Radley at rackets and represented the school at cross-country running, 1500 metres and cricket. He was good enough to represent Southampton University at both cross-country and cricket. He had a good eye and quick feet and always pushed himself to the limits of human concentration and physical endurance.

Mikie insists he was merely average and didn't always give 100 per cent, but his father insists: 'He was a very capable all-rounder and always gave his best shot. At day school in London he took boxing and came home one day and said, "I knocked out another boy's tooth today." I said, "Good heavens, do you always do that?"

"Oh, that's nothing, I made the games master's nose bleed last week!" So you see he's always had this determined streak. Prep school taught him how to work but he really blossomed at public school. There were so many things he could do. He became deputy head of school, captain of his house for a year, captain of rackets for about three years.

'I watched him playing rackets at Marlborough once. He was captaining the first string and when they had finished, after a very competitive match, he suddenly went off. I said, "Where are you going?" and he replied, "Didn't you know? I'm captain of squash as well and we start in a few minutes."

'He was always doing that sort of thing. Once he was playing cricket for Radley and he beckoned a chap off the boundary to take his place in the field. He went off and ran the mile for Radley and then came back and continued the game of cricket.'

Mikie was always pushing, pushing, pushing because he wanted to be the best and if he couldn't be the best he would 'kill' himself trying. One of his close friends once told me: 'Even without God's help Mikie would have toughed it out with his disability and illness. He is a born fighter and brave, so brave.'

In the beginning, when Mikie's life was unfolding with all the vibrancy and speed of a steeplechase, his dreams were powered by sheer mortal belief and determination to be better than the next man. 'I guess I did push myself, too hard at times,' he admitted. 'I was not afraid of hard work. There was one time, during my army career, when I was on a diet of grapefruit and other low fat food to enable me to keep my weight down so I could make the weight for a National Hunt race.

'At five feet eleven I was quite tall for a jockey so I had to keep a careful watch on my weight. I did not eat much at all and ended up quite ill. It all backfired on me during a cross-country race for the army, not many months before my accident at Huntingdon. I was leading and I knew there was one other good runner in the race and we were battling it out.

'I went ahead, I think after about five miles of a six-mile race, and that's the last thing I remember. I blacked out and collapsed because I had not been eating properly and I was pushing myself and ended up in hospital. It was bound to happen really. I was always dieting. My natural weight was about eleven and a half stone but the lowest I could do was nine stone twelve. I was always running and I guess I just overdid it, but even then I didn't learn the lesson. As soon as I had recovered I started pushing myself again.'

Between school and university Mikie entered the army on a short-service limited commission and requested to be stationed at Larkhill so he could ride the horses on Salisbury Plain. It was a dream come true for a horse-mad young man whose horsemanship was being noted, especially after his point-to-point win on Tintagel at Larkhill a year earlier, but still there was no escape from the infamously tough basic training, even though he was genuine officer material.

After receiving his commission at Sandhurst he was sent to Plymouth with the rest of the 29 Commando Regiment recruits in the summer of 1977. They got him fit, mentally and physically, but it wasn't for the faint-hearted and Mikie suffered. Strangely, he turned to the Bible for help. Coming from a family who, despite being regarded as 'God-fearing' people, kept true religion at arm's length, this wasn't particularly normal behaviour. Like many ex-public schoolboys Mikie believed in God, got confirmed, and did not wholly resent compulsory attendance at chapel. The possibility of a living, life-changing relationship with God, though, was completely alien to him. He was an intelligent, fun-loving guy who believed in God and went to church from time to time. But no matter how far removed he was from the reality of being committed as a believer, the seeds of faith had been sown in his heart and soul and Mikie suddenly realized that when things got bad he knew enough to think about God.

He was giving his all for 29 Commando Regiment, but it wasn't always enough and they wanted more. During a pre-Commando course his hands were torn to pieces, and now he lay exhausted on his bunk and started to read his standard issue army Bible. It was more out of duty than any sense of divine instruction but it worked. 'It gave me strength and helped me carry on,' he recalls. 'Maybe my motives were wrong because I thought perhaps if I read my Bible God will help me, but He did anyway.'

A broken ankle ended his training in 1978 but two years later he achieved a 2:1 Honours degree in Classics. These years also firmly established the competitive riding career of Michael Heaton-Ellis. He had become an outstanding horseman and at this moment his whole life was an exciting adventure about to unfold in any number of directions.

He left Southampton University intent on serving his five years in the army before concentrating on training racehorses. He instructed his father, who by now had retired from active service, and mother, who answered the telephone at home, to accept every ride he was offered.

On Sir Jaffa, his father's horse, Mikie enjoyed some successful forays into eventing, qualifying for the prestigious Badminton Horse Trials just one week before his fateful accident. His best result was in 1979 when he came ninth in the International Class at Wyle Horse Trials.

He recalls: 'It was my first international three-day event on the horse which my father had bought and I'd taken over. We had gone from novice to advanced and it was a real test for me. I remember it was a difficult course and we were sixty-something after the dressage on the first day, but we went fast and clear over the cross-country course and went up to ninth. Lots of people suddenly noticed that we had done well. It was quite an achievement and I think my father was particularly pleased.'

Peter Heaton-Ellis worked tirelessly behind the scenes to make sure his son had the best possible chance of success. He was more of a coach and manager than a father. 'He used to do all the fitness work because I was busy all the time,' Mikie said. 'Before I graduated I was at the university in Southampton studying most of the year and was doing army service in my holidays.

'My father used to do all the necessary preparation for events. On the actual day of competitions or three-day events he would spend the whole time with me. He would walk round the course with me and we would decide which way we were going to jump the fences. We were a good combination. Before events and races he was always right there on the other side of the horse helping me to put the saddle on, he was always part of everything.

'I was very proud of him, probably a little in awe of him as well. He has always been highly respected and trusted by everyone who knows him. He is the most upright, just and good person. He is always doing things to help others and he sticks rigidly to principles which he thinks are right.

'Even now with his antique business he doesn't think it is right that our antique furniture gets exported to America, so if he thinks a dealer is offering him a lot for furniture because it's heading for the United States he won't sell. He is very rigid like that, has very strong principles and values and he never tells a lie. He is honest through and through and my mother is the same. They are wonderful parents.'

The thing Mikie hates most about the way his life turned out, the only thing really, is what his accident did to his father and mother. They were completely devastated and have never really come to terms with the terrible, cruel twist of fate that almost completely destroyed the life of their son. 'It must have been awful for them and I felt for them a lot, because all they could do was look on.

'You know if it happens to you and you have got something to fight against, it's much easier than just looking, I think. I knew my father was strong, but in that time I saw just how strong my mother is, which had not been that apparent. They really started praying then. They had always gone to church, but they got other churches praying. Which even though they were God-fearing people was slightly out of the ordinary because they were quite conservative in their own personal faith.

'The bad thing was that when prayer did not appear to be working, although I now know God was working behind the scenes to heal me, my father, in desperation, turned to faith healers and spiritualists for help. It was not very Christian but we were clasping at straws really. I was not a believer at that time but I had an uneasy feeling about it all.

'I thought it was a bit odd really. I was myself determined to get up and walk but the doctors had told me and my parents that I would not walk again, and I think my father was just searching for alternatives to conventional medicine. Like me, he would not take no for an answer. He wanted to see his son walk and ride again.'

Before the accident Mikie also managed to ride 11 National Hunt steeplechase winners and competed in a few flat races as well. People in horse racing were beginning to sit up and take notice. Peter and Pru Heaton-Ellis were frequently being congratulated on having such a fine horseman for a son, one who not only had a natural way with horses but was also a brave and tireless jockey who just couldn't stop racing.

Mikie recalls one weekend when he rode in an amateur flat race at Kempton Park on the Friday, a novice steeplechase at Stratford on the Saturday, and an advanced one-day event in Devon on the Sunday. The last was only possible thanks to a girlfriend who had gone on ahead to get the horse ready – the same girlfriend who was with Mikie at Huntingdon on the day of his accident.

Had it not been for his accident, there is no doubt at all that Mikie would have become a top jockey. He possessed that great combination of being a fine horseman and good jockey, completely different qualities that together create a winning formula. But fate had other plans for Michael Heaton-Ellis. He could have been sent to the Falklands War, which started six months after his accident, or he could have had the luck of those jockeys who seem to be blessed with good fortune. Men like Tony McCoy and Carl Llewellyn.

Anthony McCoy, sometimes called Tony, often simply referred to as AP by his fellow jockeys, is a phenomenon. He won the senior jockey's title in his first year, which is unheard of, and during the writing of this book had already broken the record for the fastest 200 winners. Add to all of that a Champion Hurdle and a Gold Cup and the sum is a horseman of immortal precocity.

But you mention Michael Heaton-Ellis, Shane Broderick, and all the other jockeys seriously injured or killed in the pursuit of a winner: 'Well, it's a sobering thought,' he told me. 'Because every jockey, no matter how successful, is only one horse away from a bad fall.'

One evening in his second year in England, the prolific Irishman rode at a track in the West Country. His four horses, three of them favourites, all got turned over. After the final failure, McCoy returned to the weighing room in bad form, allegedly cursing and kicking and not wanting to hide it. Brendan Powell, one of the senior jockeys who has ridden several winners for Mikie, took him aside.

'What do you think you are doing?' demanded Powell. 'You are not long over from Ireland, you have had fantastic success and you are occasionally going to have days like this.

I have been here before and I've left this racecourse in an ambulance.' Powell wanted McCoy to get the message. He did.

During the 1998 Cheltenham Festival, McCoy had a fall that could have left him seriously paralysed or killed him. I remember watching the race on live television and being shocked by the ferocity and speed of McCoy's tumble. His horse jumped early and went through the top of the fence, sending McCoy somersaulting through the air and down onto the turf where he lay curled up like some wounded animal in the path of a dozen jumping horses. McCoy just made himself small and waited for them to land. There is nothing lucky about horseshoes when they're raining down like hammers on the end of three-quarters of a ton of racehorse. McCoy might as well have been sitting in a deckchair in the middle of the M27. He was clipped twice but, incredibly, most of the chasing field missed him and he walked off the course, gathered his composure and rode in his next race.

'Any time you walk to your car at the end of the day, that's not a bad day,' he said, remembering those less fortunate and the thin line between life and death, dented pride and paralysis – the reason why each one of us should never forget: 'There but for the grace of God go I.'

Depending on how you look at it, Carl Llewellyn has either been very lucky or very unlucky during his accident-prone career. He is still alive, still riding and still walking. Those jockeys who are extreme examples of how a fall can shatter a life will look at Llewellyn and his two wonderful moments of racing glory and realize that the line between their bad luck and his bad luck is so painfully thin it is hardly a line at all.

Llewellyn has ridden the winner of the Grand National twice: Party Politics in 1992 and Earth Summit in 1998. Yet even in the glorious moment of both Aintree victories, the savage effect which injury can have on a jump jockey's career and life made itself evident. Earth Summit's regular rider was Tom Jenks, who would have ridden the horse in the race had he not been on crutches after a fall. Andy Adam's place in history was denied him when a broken leg forced him off the back of Party Politics six years earlier.

Fate can be extremely cruel, but Llewellyn has tempted it all his professional career and largely escaped in one piece. His medical records make gruesome reading: broken jaw and right cheekbone; broken left forearm; compound fracture of right ankle; hairline fracture of left wrist; dislocated elbow; broken left collarbone; broken left ankle; broken right ankle; broken right foot; fractured vertebrae.

Two weeks after the 1998 Grand National I asked Llewellyn for his view about how fate can deal its hand. I told him that I had watched his win on Earth Summit from the comfort of Michael Heaton-Ellis's living-room. Mikie had actually tipped Earth Summit to win, which led me to question his claim that 'trainers make bad tipsters', although as far as I know he didn't actually have a flutter.

Anyway I said to Llewellyn: 'Sitting there with Mikie, it really hit home how cruel fate can be. I mean, had things worked out differently for him as a promising young jockey he could have been riding in the National. How does it make you feel when you see ex-jockeys badly hurt, crippled or killed? Does it place a chill in your heart? Does it make you want to quit while you are still in one piece?'

Silence. Carl was searching his soul. Finally he answered: 'No, I don't even think about it. I just do my job, sometimes I get hurt, most of the time I don't, but I'm always grateful when I get home in one piece. No one wants to get hurt and no one likes to see others getting hurt, but it doesn't stop me enjoying what I do. I love it. Of course if you have a bad fall you might think, "That's it, I've had enough," but you can't recall pain and as you heal you forget.'

McCoy feels much the same way, but he was at Richard Davis's funeral and it had a profound effect on him. Not enough to make him think of quitting because like Llewellyn, McCoy is a consummate professional. He is fully aware of the dangers, but accepts them in the same way he accepts that fate deals its hand any way it chooses. I like guys like McCoy and Llewellyn because of their honesty, and this is the good part: they don't feel sorry for Mikie, they are inspired by him.

'He is very well thought of,' Peter Heaton-Ellis said. 'But he always has been. When he had the accident Mikie was terribly worried that he'd dropped out of everything, but they wouldn't allow that. The top people in horse racing visited him, even the Queen Mother sent her private secretary to see him.

'Jockeys used to visit him in hospital all the time and at the first race meeting he went to after his accident, at Newbury, he was presented with a book signed by all the jockeys. They kept him in the business, and he hasn't looked back. The sad thing is that he had the ability to be a top jockey and I am sure he would have been very successful, but still he hasn't done too badly for himself.'

4
. . . .

Finding and Believing

If you want to get ahead in life it sometimes helps to have friends in high places, or at least the right places. To repeat a well-known phrase: it's not what you know but who you know. In this respect, Michael Heaton-Ellis is lucky. He is very well connected, although to his credit he has worked hard to make the right connections. Among his mentors are men like Henry Cecil, Richard Hannon and John Dunlop, three of the most respected trainers in British horse racing. And of course there is Sheikh Mohammed bin Rashid Al Maktoum, the most powerful figure in the history of the thoroughbred industry and one of Mikie's biggest admirers.

In keeping with his whole attitude to life, Michael Heaton-Ellis never let go of his dream to train racehorses but equally left nothing to chance. His faith may be the substance of things unseen but his career has been built on tangible foundations and meticulously planned. Ten years of hard work in an already hard game laid the foundations for his arrival at Barbury Castle almost a decade ago and by the time he collected his trainer's licence from the Jockey Club at Portman Square at the age of 32, nine years after his accident, he possessed the kind of exclusive knowledge and understanding about his chosen profession that many trainers starting out on their own would sell their souls for.

'I have had the best training, having worked with a lot of gifted trainers,' he said. 'I have been very fortunate, in some respects, although I knew what I wanted and how to get it and would not settle for anything less than the best training, and even though after I became a Christian I realized that God has been pulling the strings and opening doors for me to fulfil my dream to train racehorses. He has made it possible but I owe a lot to the people who have helped me along the way.'

Mikie's training started once he left the spinal injury unit at Stoke Mandeville, Aylesbury, paralysed from the chest down, ten months after that fateful day at Huntingdon. As a result of Brough Scott and John Oaksey, of the Injured Jockey Fund, visiting him in hospital, Mikie learned that Sam Sheppard, the then secretary of the Thoroughbred Breeders Association, was looking for an assistant. It wasn't what he really wanted to do but he took the job in the strong belief that if he was going to be a successful trainer he needed to know about breeding.

It turned out to be a crucial move that would eventually convert Michael to flat racing. For two years he travelled around the stud farms and sales of Britain's flat-racing industry and by the end of that time he knew without a shadow of a doubt that what he wanted to do was train these beautiful thoroughbred young horses to be the best and fastest they could be. He loved their speed and athleticism and discovered, to his joy, that he had a natural eye for a horse, 'a gift from God' as he would later claim.

Though confined to a wheelchair he had discovered a sport in which he would play a full and active part, and everyone who really mattered felt the same way. By August 1982 he had learnt to look after himself, and left hospital bolstered by the support of the racing industry and men like Scott and Oaksey, as well as other top racing people who were bowled over by the courage and determination of a man who had made up his mind not to leave Stoke Mandeville unless he could do so on his feet. Eventually he did, but only with the help of crutches and calipers, because no matter how hard he tried or how strongly he believed in the power of his own iron will, Mikie was crippled. He was paralysed and, barring a miracle, it was permanent.

'I was determined to make the most of muscles I could use and also be independent,' he said, with a touch of irony in his voice after learning that motor neurone disease will destroy the last functioning muscles in his body and take away his independence, unless God defies medical opinion. 'When I left hospital,' he recalls, 'I lived on my own and learned how to live as normally as possible with a wheelchair as my constant companion. I vowed to make the best use of my life.

'When Brough Scott and John Oaksey of the Injured Jockey Fund came to see me in Stoke Mandeville I said, 'Look, I don't want any money. I just want help to get a job in racing.'

It provided the opening he needed and brought an introduction to Bob McCreery, then president of the Thoroughbred Breeders Association, and a subsequent interview at Newmarket gained him the post of assistant to Sam Sheppard. It wasn't the route Mikie had planned to take but as things turned out it was the perfect start for a budding young trainer, although at that time he would have given anything to be back in the saddle and winning races over fences or riding the gunner's horse on Salisbury Plain. At the age of 23 he never expected his career as a jockey or army officer to be over.

'If it had not been for my accident I would have stayed in the army for another five years at least. That's the amount of time I agreed to do to pay the army back for my university scholarship, and maybe I would have stayed in longer than that, who knows. My next job in the army would have been a Section Commander in the King's Troop. The only mounted unit in the gunners and the regiment my father used to command.

'I always thought I was going to be a trainer after being a jockey but I didn't know how I was going to do it. One of my friends, James Beazeley, who I shared a house with at university and is now Chief Executive of the British Bloodstock Agency at Newmarket, always said to me, "I can't understand why if you want to be a jockey you don't go and ride out and work for a really big yard and try to get really into racing." But the answer was because I was also planning to do more event riding as well.

'So probably I think I would have ended up doing my five years in the army and at the same time continued riding in National Hunt races and eventing to gain experience, and I probably would have left the army at the age of 28 and gone off to try and be a full-time jockey and then graduate to being a trainer. The stumbling block was always money, and it is the big problem facing anyone who wants to start up as a trainer with their own yard, unless they are very rich.

'It's a great irony that my accident solved this problem because I was well insured and got enough money to set me up financially. With money in the bank I was able to concentrate on learning the ropes and start planning my future as a potential trainer.'

Being at Newmarket, Mikie could go to the gallops on his four-wheeled motorbike and watch the horses work, and that enabled him to get closely involved with the local stables. 'I made a lot of good contacts and was learning all the time. I used to go out early morning to watch Henry Cecil's and other trainers' horses gallop on the heath at Newmarket before I went to the office of the Breeding Association. There was a lot of office work, things like researching bloodstock, not so much travelling around, but I still managed to get out to horse sales and see what was happening.

'I used to take my holidays and spend them looking at horses and learning about buying horses, especially yearlings.

I was thirsty for knowledge; what it was that made a good horse, what to look out for, et cetera. I met my wife Katie at the horse sales in Ireland and shared with her my dream of becoming a trainer. It really was a good time for me.'

In his second year at the headquarters of British horse racing, Mikie went to see his friend Henry Cecil and, having had moments of doubt himself, asked the champion trainer, 'Can you think of any reasons why I can't train?' To which Cecil answered, 'No, I can't.'

Mikie later recalled: 'Henry did think about my question for a minute. I wondered if he was going to say, "Well, actually there are several reasons why you can't train," but he didn't. What he actually said was, "Mikie, you can do everything that I do. I don't go out and physically feed the horses, I don't go out and ride them so I don't see why you can't."

'I said, "It's always been my ambition but I wanted confirmation that I can do the job properly despite my disability. I have had my doubts." '

Maybe it was more fear than doubt, because Mikie had realized quite soon that as a trainer you physically don't have to ride horses, and that was the only thing he couldn't do. Training is mostly done through the eyes, just watching. Mikie knew he had a way with horses, a natural ability to identify their strengths and weaknesses. Deep down he knew he could train but he wanted to test his theory. That's why he went to see his hero at that time, Henry Cecil.

He reassured Mikie, saying, 'I am a hundred per cent certain you can, but how are you going to go about it?'

Cecil knew the pitfalls facing an ambitious young trainer like Mikie and they had nothing to do with the fact that he was paralysed. What really worried Cecil was the harsh economic climate of racehorse training. More experienced men than Mikie had been blown away because they simply could not make it pay. It was a huge gamble, but Cecil wanted to see Mikie succeed, which is quite rare in a sport where rivalry between trainers is incredibly fierce and newcomers are usually discouraged.

Mikie trusted Cecil, and in return the man who has dominated horse racing for years and years backed his remarks up by getting the wheels in motion for Mikie to move into the often cut-throat but still hugely fulfilling business. 'Have you got a plan?' he asked.

'Well, I'm going to be an assistant trainer first,' Mikie replied.

'Where are you going to train?' Cecil continued, half expecting Mikie's answer.

'Newmarket, I guess,' came the reply. Cecil's face broke into a wry smile. He knew Mikie lived in Newmarket and knew it would be a big mistake for him to launch his career there.

'If I was you,' he said, 'I would go and be an assistant trainer somewhere else. Your first job should really be away from Newmarket so you can go and make your mistakes somewhere else and then come back. It's the best way.'

Cecil knew that his close friend and fellow trainer John Dunlop was looking for an assistant, so he agreed to write to Dunlop suggesting Mikie would be the ideal man for the job. The man in charge of the biggest training operation in England at that time agreed and after two years at Newmarket, Mikie moved to Sussex as assistant to Dunlop at the training stable at beautiful Arundel Castle.

In contrast to the rather eccentric Cecil, who followed his father-in-law, Sir Noel Murless, as master of the famous Warren Place yard at Newmarket and served a four-year apprenticeship as assistant to his stepfather Sir Cecil Boyd-Rochfort, Dunlop has no background in professional racing, being the son of a country doctor. But in 1966 at the age of 27, following two assistant training jobs, he opened up the historic Arundel yard to the public ownership of horses, a yard formerly used as a private establishment for the Duke and Duchess of Norfolk.

Cecil, who has landed the trainer's championship nine times since 1976, and Dunlop, who came top in 1995, do share one thing in common, however. They are both incredibly laid back. In Dunlop's case this image tends to disguise one of racing's keenest brains. His skill in improving horses after their first run is well known in the game and his record of winning top events abroad is second to none. In 1987 Dunlop saddled the winners of 61 races worth £403,000 in this country but during the same period won for his clients £603,000 overseas.

Mikie had wed equestrian artist Katie O'Sullivan six months before he started work at Dunlop's impressive yard at the beginning of 1985. He bought a thatched cottage six miles from Arundel Castle in the picturesque village of Watersfield, and in such a large, smooth-running operation he loved the work and learned quickly. 'John has always been one of the top trainers in the country and still is. He had over 200 horses and that meant more horses for me to look at, more jobs to do and more responsibility. It was a good place to work and although John had two assistants and I was starting at the bottom as a student, he looked after me really well and went out of his way to show me the ropes.'

Dunlop, one of the top three trainers in England at that time, hired Mikie during a boom time for the Arundel yard, but ironically his first year coincided with a particularly nasty virus that forced Dunlop to close his whole yard down with no runners for more than a month, and Mikie found himself looking after sick horses rather than learning how to train prime-condition thoroughbred winners.

His days were spent monitoring temperatures, taking them twice a day and recording any changes, and endoscoping to check for mucus, because the virus that visited Arundel in the winter of 1985 attacked the respiratory system making it impossible for Dunlop's horses to train properly. 'It was a very bad time for John,' Mikie recalls, 'but it was good for me because in that short time I learned a lot about the care and treatment of sick horses.'

Barbury Castle has had its own share of sick horses but Mikie's experience at Arundel prepared him. He also studied with professors and doctors on equine biology and hygiene. 'It stood me in good stead because if you are going to be a successful trainer it is vital to know how to protect your yard against illness,' he said, 'and if you are unfortunate enough to get a bad cold running through your yard you have to know how to deal with it. It doesn't make you a successful trainer but proper hygiene should give a healthy horse.'

Eventually Dunlop's yard recovered, and Mikie was able to get on with the task of learning the ropes of actually training and placing horses in races, which he was especially good at. 'John gave me a lot of responsibility, especially at his other yard at Findon where I spent quite a lot of time.'

The Sussex town of Findon is just down the road from Arundel and once the home of racing legend Captain Ryan Price, famous for his good placing of handicappers and furiously backing his own judgement with the bookmakers, something which Mikie would rarely do because of his belief, shared with many of his colleagues, that trainers make bad tipsters. Price was generally an exception to the rule.

Dunlop stabled 160 of his horses at Arundel with the rest at Findon, and Mikie's working week was split between the two yards and on the two tried and trusted gallops; one for everyday cantering work and one for fast work, twice a week. It's a similar pattern to how Mikie trains at Barbury Castle except that whereas Dunlop only ever used two gallops, Mikie has enormous variety on the vast land around his yard on the Marlborough Downs.

'Variety is good,' he says, 'but it is much easier to monitor a horse's progress if you are using the same gallops all the time. People often comment on how wonderful it must be to have so many gallops and hills to train my horses, but John had only a fraction of what I've got at Barbury and yet he was incredibly successful.'

One of the reasons, albeit a small reason, why Dunlop's horses enjoyed continued success during Mikie's two years at Arundel and Findon was his knack of placing runners. It is one of Mikie's strengths as a trainer. He looks at the form and fitness of a horse and instinctively knows which race the horse should run in to give it the best possible chance of success. Once he had been in Dunlop's employment long enough to prove this ability, Mikie began to help place horses in the right races three weeks in advance, which is a world of difference from today's five-day entry rule that gives trainers a much better chance of getting it right.

Back in 1985, Mikie was placing horses in races 21 days before they were scheduled to run, but more often than not he got it right, which is why he ended up being headhunted for one of the top jobs in horse racing.

In 1984 Mikie persuaded his then mother-in-law Claire O'Sullivan to buy a yearling filly. In its first year, after being given the name Sweet Domain, the horse was affected by the virus that forced Dunlop to close down his yard for part of the 1985 season, but still showed promise and got placed. In its second year Mikie entered Sweet Domain in a race at Redcar despite strong opposition from Dunlop, who believed it would be waste of time and money. 'She's unlikely to get placed and it's such a bloody long way to go to end up empty handed,' he said.

But Mikie would not take no for an answer because he had a gut feeling that Sweet Domain would win, and she did. Later, at a Newmarket dinner party, Sweet Domain's success at Redcar came up in a conversation between Dunlop and an influential member of the thoroughbred racing fraternity, Anthony Stroud, Sheikh Mohammed's racing manager. Stroud, who knew Mikie, inquired about the form of Claire O'Sullivan's filly, to which Dunlop replied, 'Oh, she won at Redcar, didn't you hear?'

'Well done,' Stroud replied, 'I bet Mikie is pleased.'

'Yes, he is, but it's entirely down to him that Sweet Domain did it because I told Mikie that she wasn't up to it. But he's good at placing horses and he's shaping up to be a good trainer.'

Stroud smiled. He knew what Dunlop said was true because he had already been told to keep an eye on Michael Heaton-Ellis. He didn't know it at the time, but Sweet Domain's win at unfashionable Redcar in the north-east of England would become a factor in helping Mikie get a job working for the most powerful figure in the history of the thoroughbred industry.

The original plan was to work for Dunlop for three years but after two Stroud asked Mikie to join Sheikh Mohammed's racing team. 'Initially I didn't want to do it. I didn't want to manage racehorses, but at the same time it was an opportunity that shouldn't be missed,' he said.

It certainly wasn't an offer to be turned down, with more than 500 horses scattered throughout the world and 28 top trainers to deal with, and looking back Mikie admits he probably would have lived to regret declining the invitation.

Sheikh Mohammed bin Rashid Al Maktoum, crown prince of oil-rich Dubai and defence minister of the United Arab Emirates, had for several months received glowing reports about a gifted young former army officer and jockey by the name of Michael Heaton-Ellis. He had heard that this man, confined to a wheelchair following a tragic accident, had a wonderful eye for a horse and a natural affinity with the beautiful creatures that are so very important in the life of a man who values horses more than all the riches in his kingdom.

Every thoroughbred alive is descended from one of three Arab stallions, two of which provide the names for Sheikh Mohammed's racing company, Darley Stud Management, and the Godolphin operation which Mikie's former employer set up after becoming tired of dealing with trainers who made him feel that his only important function was to pay the bills.

Godolphin began its worldwide plundering of the Turf's major prizes in 1993, six years after Sheikh Mohammed hired an ambitious 29-year-old Michael Heaton-Ellis as a racing manager, and since Balanchine followed her win in the 1994 Oaks at Epsom with victory in the Irish Derby, Godolphin's blue colours have been carried to unprecedented success around the globe.

Rather ironically Mikie almost came to blows with the man who was instrumental in setting up the Godolphin Organization, Jeremy Noseda. He was one of the assistants to Dunlop at Arundel Castle during Mikie's two-year spell in Sussex, but the pair did not see eye to eye. They were meant to share the responsibility of filling in the entry book for Dunlop but could never agree on which horse should run where.

Noseda had been working for Dunlop for a few years, and may well have resented the young trainer who had only recently arrived at Arundel but was rapidly beginning to prove himself as an astute judge of form. One night, following a heated argument in Dunlop's office, Noseda stormed out and vindictively snapped the aerial on Mikie's car before getting into his own car and racing out of the yard and down to the local pub.

Enraged, Mikie got in his own car and went to find Noseda. He spotted Noseda's car parked outside the pub and in an act of vengeance tore off its aerial. Mikie drove off and turned around to head back to his home in Watersfield but Noseda had already seen him and ran out of the pub and into the road, where he stood armed with a pint glass. Mikie carried on driving but Noseda was crazy with anger and threw the glass at the moving vehicle. Fortunately for Mikie it bounced off the windscreen without shattering the glass.

Noseda eventually quit, but not before Mikie left Arundel. After working for John Gosden, one of Sheikh Mohammed's personal trainers, he linked up with Simon Crisford, who was to replace Mikie after he quit as a racing manager for the Sheikh, and together, with the help of renowned trainer Saeed Bin Suroor, they launched Godolphin. Noseda, who vaguely remembers his heated clash with Mikie, is now running his own racing stables at Newmarket following a stint in the United States.

In 1995, as Mikie was putting the wealth of valuable experience and contacts he had gained from his three seasons as one of Sheikh Mohammed's racing managers to good use in the promotion of his own stables, Godolphin horses mounted successful raids at top races in Britain, France, Hong Kong, Ireland, Italy, Japan and the United States. Mikie, who by this time was firmly established as a trainer in his own right, could watch with a certain amount of satisfaction every time one of the Sheikh's horses won a major race. Part of the foundations of the Godolphin Organization had been laid by the hard work of men like Michael Heaton-Ellis who toiled behind the scenes to make sure the crown prince of Dubai's horses were almost always without equal.

But in October 1995 Sheikh Mohammed shocked British racing. The head of the Godolphin Organization decided to relocate all of the 40 horses he had with Henry Cecil, citing the knee problem that had afflicted the impressive Mark of Esteem before the Royal Lodge Stakes at Ascot a month earlier as crucial to his drastic action.

Mikie felt sorry for Cecil who had been so supportive to him in the past, but there was a lesson to be learned, or rather reinforced. Cecil, one of the best trainers in England, had upset and lost the trust of his most important owner and paid a heavy price. It was a reminder to Mikie of the unpredictable and volatile climate of his new world.

If Sheikh Mohammed shocked British racing then, two and a half years later in April 1998, Mikie's former employer completely terrified the industry by announcing his intention to relocate to France at the year's end a substantial part of his powerful Godolphin operation. The move will cause pain, grief and loss of jobs – particularly in Newmarket.

Back in December 1997 Mikie told me that this could happen. Sheikh Mohammed warned bluntly in his pre-Christmas Gimcrack Speech that unless prize money in British horse racing was increased his equine forces would decamp. 'Is he serious?' I asked. 'Yes,' said Mikie, 'he's threatened to pull out before and I think one day he'll do it.'

It's a sad fact that Britain, founder of thoroughbred racing 300 years ago, now scrapes the bottom of the pile of the world's racing countries in rewards-to-costs ratio. The reason is simple. Alone of the world's main racing countries, we, quite insanely, allow bookmakers to operate both on and off the course. Their profits – in the case of the big chains millions of pounds annually – are not returned to racing. In France, as everywhere on the Continent and in the United States, profit from betting goes not to shareholders or other business ventures – much of Ladbroke's profits have been spent on hotels and in America – but to the Government and back into racing.

French prize money is often two or three times bigger than ours. It spreads right down the line, so there is also a real threat that Arab studs now in England might move to France. The worry for trainers like Mikie is that the Godolphin move will alert many more owners to the advantages of French racing, although it could bring a smile to the face of his old adversary Jeremy Noseda.

At the time of writing the Godolphin plan is to buy the ultra-modern but disused Evry racecourse south of Paris. The trainers Sheikh Mohammed employs in France will be required to pass a written French exam. It is easier now, though, because candidates can sit the test with the aid of an interpreter. The previous system had prevented the non-French speaking Noseda from setting up in France. I bet the air was blue.

Working for Sheikh Mohammed, back when Noseda was pre-occupied with other things, Mikie's particular job was to place the finest horses in the world in the right races. This meant careful liaison with trainers and was a wonderful apprenticeship for the aspiring trainer. 'I am very interested in the placing of horses to win races, putting them in the right place to win, and the job also enabled me to watch the best trainers in the world operating,' he said. 'I saw their routine with the horses, the way they are trained, the way they are fed and how they deal with the problems.'

It would be wrong to suggest that Mikie had some kind of exclusive relationship with Sheikh Mohammed or that his position was anything more than that of a small cog in a large well-oiled machine. After all, he never enjoyed the privilege of visiting Dubai where the famous Al Quoz training centre is situated, along with the most advanced stabling and equine hospital in the world, a mere stone's throw from Sheikh Mohammed's Za'abeel Palace.

Very few young trainers have travelled the world like Mikie has, but his three years working under the guidance of Sheikh Mohammed's racing manager Anthony Stroud were nowhere near as glamorous as they may appear. The lifestyle suited Mikie but every hour of ego-boosting glitz was paid for by many more hours of plain old sweat. Of course, he had his hand-controlled BMW and carphone and occasionally jetted around the world, always staying in the best hotels, with a group of glamorous women around him, but the assumption that Michael Heaton-Ellis became a made man during his time on the payroll of the most powerful figure in horse racing is nothing more than a fancy myth.

'My salary was okay and I had a taste of the high life, but it wasn't all it's cracked up to be,' he told me. 'I used to fly around Europe to watch the Sheikh's horses run, but more often than not I would go there and back in one day to cut down on the cost and time involved.

'I did stay in the best hotels and there was a bit of glamour attached to the job. I took good holidays to exotic destinations, but most of the time I was just a number on the payroll of a large organization that made a lot of money and did not cut corners when it came to paying expenses. If I had to stay overnight it would be in the best hotel available and one year I went to the Kentucky sales in the United States. I flew first-class which I'd never done before.

'The Sheikh gave me money to buy a car but I actually asked him if I could make up the difference out of my own pocket to buy the BMW I had always wanted, so you see there wasn't a bottomless pot of money. The job wasn't complete extravagance and the work was hard and mostly very unglamorous. I was told it would be tough and it was.'

It was Stroud who warned Mikie of the amount of work involved in the job of racing manager for Sheikh Mohammed, but he also polished up the flip side of the coin, selling Mikie the glamour and the travel and of course the money, and the beautiful women who are part and parcel of the international horse racing jet-set.

Mikie spent most of his employment for the Sheikh based at Newmarket which is where he was initially sounded out by Stroud, who was eager to hire the man who was making a name for himself as John Dunlop's assistant.

'I was working for John at the sales at Newmarket one day when I was approached by Anthony Stroud. He sold the job to me and I felt that despite my initial doubts about getting into managing as opposed to training, which is what I really wanted to do, the job would be a brilliant way of learning from watching other trainers, because at that time the Sheikh had twenty-eight different trainers around the world and I would be working with all of them, so I thought yeah, I'll do it. I got back to Anthony and said, "OK, you've convinced me, but I won't commit myself to more than three years because I want to actually train horses myself."'

So Mikie said thanks and goodbye to John Dunlop and went to work for Sheikh Mohammed bin Rashid Al Maktoum. For the best part of two years, 1987 to 1989, he watched the finest horses in the world, writing reports on every gallop and every race before faxing them to the Sheikh. In the relatively small world of thoroughbred racing he got to know everyone and more importantly got known. In the space of seven years, the young horseman whose dream to train race-horses seemed to have been shattered on that track at Huntingdon had become somebody, and yet he wanted more.

In his mind he could already see a wooden sign that said 'Michael Heaton-Ellis – Trainer' pointing the way to a future where he believed his dream would come true, not on streets paved with the Sheikh's gold but on a gravel road of raw desire. Barbury Castle shone like a beacon in the hazy distance of Mikie's future.

5
#######

Learning How to Trust

Luca Cumani, the charismatic Italian who has trained thoroughbreds at Newmarket since the mid-1970s, once said that a trainer of racehorses is more the master of his own destiny in England than in any other country. Nowhere else in the world, he said, is training racehorses such an exciting and attractive occupation, and you perform best when you are happy.

Mikie wasn't completely fulfilled at John Dunlop's yards at Arundel Castle and Findon and his heart and soul certainly wasn't always in his work for Sheikh Mohammed, whether he was at Newmarket or in Europe, Australia, New Zealand, South Africa, anywhere. What he wanted more than anything was a place of his own.

Cumani has a simple theory about the pulling power of running a stable in England. The reason why we have so many good trainers in this country, he said, is that here it is a lovely job.

Mikie did not need convincing. He had seen the difference between training conditions in Europe and the United States and longed to enjoy the same lifestyle as trainers such as Cumani and Cecil who, with their individual yards and the use of such a wide range of gallops and canters at Newmarket, are richly blessed compared with their counterparts in other

64

countries, where trainers are crowded into the stabling area at racetracks and obliged to exercise their animals on the same surface used for racing.

After spending many hours studying the form of horses on the Newmarket Heath gallops and at racecourses around Britain, and being fascinated by the raw athleticism of the yearlings at horse sales during the time between working for the Thoroughbred Breeders Association and joining Sheikh Mohammed's racing team, Mikie fell in love with the idea of starting his own yard.

He had always planned to become a trainer, but watching men like Cumani and Cecil and working for Dunlop intensified this desire until it burned inside him day and night. He could imagine what it would feel like to train winners and he was determined to fulfil his ambition, even though he knew giving up a well-paid job with Sheikh Mohammed and moving to a non-existent yard with no guaranteed income would be a huge gamble.

Training racehorses is a labour-intensive and very risky business at the best of times. Back in the early nineties when Mikie was waiting for his trainer's licence, racing journalist John Hoskins said that the sport has its own serial killers. Falling attendances and off-course turnover, fixture slashing and prize money cuts had been gunning the industry down. Two more trainers had lately bitten the dust, he said. Lynda Ramsden – who is now back in business and thriving – and John Wilson had been blown away because they simply could not make it pay. So why did Michael Heaton-Ellis think he could succeed where others had failed?

It was a fair question and Mikie, more than most, knew that Hoskins had a point. If he wasn't very careful he too could end up being blown away. The odds on his dream turning into a nightmare were probably quite long, and Mikie had

seen problems inflicted on Cecil and Cumani and many others including Newmarket trainer and close friend Alex Scott.

Cecil suffered when Sheikh Mohammed relocated his 40
horses, while Cumani, who learned the ropes as Cecil's assistant during the mid-1970s, was hit by a serious recession and
the loss of the same number of well-bred horses from his
care through the Aga Khan's decision in December 1990 to
concentrate his racing interests in France.

Cecil and Cumani lost precious horses but Scott lost his
life. He was killed in a shooting incident involving another
man in the autumn of 1994.

It sounds terribly callous but Mikie actually felt a sense
of relief when he heard that Scott had been murdered. The
reason for this rather shocking reaction to the news of the death
of his friend was that Mikie feared Scott had taken his own life.
'He was a manic depressive and it was almost a relief that someone else had done it,' he said, remembering the moment when
he first heard the awful news. 'I was driving home from London
one night, it was one or two in the morning and I wasn't really
with it, and there was a news flash on the radio saying this racehorse trainer at Newmarket has been found dead – shot!
I thought, "Oh no, he's killed himself," but he hadn't. I felt
numb inside. He was a very, very great friend of mine.'

The pair went back a long way. Alex Scott was the godson
of Mikie's mother Pru and his father is the godfather of Mikie's
sister Charlotte, creating strong family ties. Mikie, a year older
than Alex, can recall a time when they rode in point-to-point
races together, especially the day when Alex's horse almost
killed him during a steeplechase at Larkhill. It was during their
student days: Mikie was studying Classics at Southampton
while Alex was reading Theology at Cambridge.

Mikie: 'I was offered a ride on another horse and got Alex
to ride the horse I was supposed to ride. I had to drag him

away from a party in Cambridge to get him to take the ride, but in the end I almost wished I hadn't gone to so much trouble because my horse fell and his horse landed straight on top of me. I hurt my back and remember feeling very relieved when I could move my legs.'

Scott, like Mikie, became a trainer. He was employed by Sheikh Maktoum, Sheikh Mohammed's older brother, to train some of the finest horses in racing out of Newmarket, having enjoyed a successful first season in 1989. He was exceptionally good at his job and looked destined to stay at the top for a long time.

But behind the cool, suave exterior, there were problems. To see Alex Scott, with his swarthy good looks and boyish charm, puffing away at his favourite brand of cigar you would not have guessed that he was a man who often could not cope with life. He came in at the top where the pressure is greater than the rewards on offer to those who have the nerve to gamble their sanity. But Scott had a history of depression and he had already caved in once as he crammed for his finals at Cambridge. Now the stakes were much higher and he frequently confessed to Mikie that he was struggling to stay on top of things.

Mikie: 'I tried to spend a lot of time with him talking and sharing about my faith. There were times when we talked a lot. As far as I could see, he never actually committed himself to follow God but when he was very down he thought about it a lot.

'I remember when I was assistant to Richard Hannon and Alex was in his second or third year as a trainer, I drove down to Newmarket to see him. He was very depressed, everything was getting on top of him, his whole life really. I told him that God was the real answer to his problems. He said, "I can't make any decisions what to do," but I think he started to realize that there was some truth in what I was saying.

'In the end he came to stay with me for a while to try and sort himself out. He went to stay with another friend in Ireland before returning to Newmarket for medication. I think he was taking lithium.'

Lithium carbonate is used relatively rarely in cases of manic depression but for certain individuals it can make a dramatic difference to their lives, releasing them from the severe mood swings which are so common in manic depression.

The real tragedy, though, was that Alex Scott was over his depression, or at the very least in control of it, when he was killed. The drugs were working and according to Mikie Alex was in 'brilliant form' during the months leading up to his death. The pair had spent the previous day together at Newmarket races. Mikie had a winner – a horse called Try to Please owned by one of Alex's clients – and had watched the race with Alex's wife Julia.

The next time he saw her was at the funeral. She had asked him to give a reading and Mikie used the same text which Alex had read from at his father's funeral some years earlier. It was a terrible day for Julia Scott and the rest of Alex's family, for Mikie, and for horse racing in general. It could have happened to anyone, but in the cold light of day there was no disguising the fact that Alex Scott had been a victim of his own success.

The bare facts of his tragic death point to a simple case of wounded pride and jealous rage. Scott was shot by a man who worked for him at the stud he had bought at Cheveley, near Newmarket. The stud groom was virtually running the place when Scott took over and could not cope with someone else telling him what to do. He feared for his job, guarding his position jealously, so he killed Scott and was later convicted of murder.

On 10 June 1995, at Epsom, a chestnut colt called Lamm-tarra, who had won only once before in his life, won the

Derby with a breathtaking run in the last two furlongs of the one-and-a-half-mile Classic to shatter the course record and provide Alex Scott with a fitting epitaph.

Scott had fallen in love with Lammtarra from the moment he started to train him, and after the horse had won a Listed race in 1994, Scott asked Mike Dillon of Ladbrokes to let him have a Derby bet of £1,000 at 33–1. When Scott was killed, technically that wager was void, but two days after Lammtarra flew past the Epsom winning post almost 12 months later, Dillon posted a cheque to Scott's widow Julia.

It was a touching gesture echoed by Lammtarra's jockey Walter Swinburn who said, 'Let's remember Alex. He was the man who believed in the horse even before the first run. I just wish he had been here to see it.' Maybe he did.

During an interview with Hugh McIlvanney for the *Observer* in March 1992, Cumani said: 'You do have to be obsessed to remain upbeat in the face of such problems, though you must be capable of maintaining a balance to avoid going round the bend. One characteristic that definitely links the leading trainers is a devouring appetite for knowledge. None of us will die knowing 10 per cent of what there is to know about the horse but we are always striving, trying to analyse our experience for indications of how we can be most effective.'

Cumani's simple philosophy appealed to Mikie, especially the theory that someone with absolute commitment, and possessing the capacity to establish a rapport with horses and a feel for each one's needs and precise abilities, can start with very little and go all the way to the top.

Cumani, though, like many top trainers, came from a thoroughbred training background. His father, the late Sergio Cumani, was Italy's champion trainer 10 times before he died at 53. Luca Cumani had connections and credentials. There was a time when Mikie had neither, but now as he assessed the pros and cons of starting his own yard he had both, and perhaps more importantly he had Jesus.

Mikie's wife Katie walked out of the marriage shortly after he joined Sheikh Mohammed's racing team but six months into the new job Mikie made a decision to commit his life to God, and set about seeking God's will for his long-term future. 'I prayed very hard about it. I understood all the dangers, and struggled to work out my motivation for wanting to have my own yard. Was it for me? Was I trying to prove something? Was I being selfish and stupid? The truth is I really felt God's hand was on the plan, so I asked Him to make it happen and He did.'

In September 1989 his prayers were answered when the call he had waited so long for came; Ian Balding, who has trained for the Queen and Sheikh Mohammed, told Mikie he knew someone called Conrad Goess at Barbury Castle with a lovely estate. He was looking for a young trainer and, in Balding's own words, 'If I wasn't at Kingsclere I would move there tomorrow.'

It was some recommendation. Balding at Kingsclere – between Newbury and Basingstoke – trained the handsome little colt Mill Reef to become the champion of his day in 1971: winner of the Derby, Eclipse, King George and Arc de Triomphe.

It was the break Mikie wanted so he went to see Goess, who is an Austrian count, and between them they started planning the yard, extra gallops and all the other parts of what would become a highly tuned racing establishment. Mikie was excited and relieved. Several doors had already slammed shut in his face and he was getting quite desperate, although it would still take a miracle to begin training on Goess's land. The count's proposal was not exactly cast in stone.

Before he got the call from Balding, Mikie was exploring other avenues. During a trip to the United States he met John Gosden, who hinted at the possibility of setting Mikie up in a yard where he could train some of the horses Gosden was planning to train for Sheikh Mohammed on his return to England from America. It was a complete non-starter, though, and Mikie looked into several other openings only to see the door close on them as well. To make matters worse he had already helped Stroud find the man who would replace him as a racing manager for Sheikh Mohammed, Simon Crisford, and suddenly he found himself in a kind of limbo with nowhere to go and nothing to do.

He recalls: 'Crisford had come in and was taking over my old job, so I was in a bit of a fix really and my prayers and thoughts were getting quite desperate. I had been a Christian for less than a year and could not understand why I had ended up in this situation where I had not got a clue what I was going to do next.

'I'd sit and pray and say, "God, I thought you wanted me to be a racehorse trainer, what's going on?" I could not see my way forward.'

Then the man who had achieved so much in horse racing in the eight years since his accident began to doubt his calling in life. It went through his mind that maybe God didn't want him to train horses. 'My attitude certainly changed towards training so I said, "OK, God, if you want me to do something different then I'll make changes, because you know I want to do it your way, not my way. I want to be in your will for my life so what would be great is if you could show me what you want me to do."'

So Mikie started looking for a sign, some kind of instruction from above, so that he could finally get some peace. It was a dangerous move because a soul in need can be easily led astray, and Mikie had already got the idea in his mind that maybe God wanted him to be a missionary. 'I started reading the papers and was expecting to see that there was a mission going to China or somewhere and they needed someone like me to work there. I was prepared to do whatever I believed God wanted me to.'

Fortunately for British horse racing Mikie never came across a vacancy for a wheelchair-bound missionary. Instead he received the call from Balding and subsequent introduction to Goess and in an act of complete madness, fuelled by sheer pig-headedness and faith, wrote to prospective owners saying: 'The Lord has given me a wonderful opportunity to train at Barbury Castle.' No one objected and a friend of Mikie even called to say, 'I thought Conrad was a count not a lord.'

That certainly brought a smile to Mikie's face but inside he was feeling slightly jittery, to say the least. There was still huge uncertainty whether Conrad Goess would actually go through with it, and Mikie knew he could end up with egg all over his face and his dream in tatters.

At that time Mikie had no idea that his faith would be tested in such an intense way, but he was about to learn how to live and trust day by day. The whole plan was covered in prayer, by Mikie and several Christian friends and family, and he is certain that this played a crucial role in getting Barbury.

The main concern of Conrad and the Goess family trust was money. They would pull the plug on the whole plan unless it was proved to be financially viable. Mikie had not really considered this, mainly because he had been carried away on the wave of enthusiasm that came rolling into his life when Balding called and set up a meeting with the man who would eventually become Mikie's landlord.

Years earlier Goess had bought Temple Farm, which is the vast estate surrounding Barbury Castle and includes all the gallops and hills that Mikie now uses to train his horses. Goess was making money renting out these gallops to local trainers so, with Balding's help, he built more gallops, but failed to increase his income because he could not find any more trainers. It was then that Balding suggested to Goess that the old farm at Barbury Castle would be a good place for someone to train. The count agreed, so they set about finding the right man.

Goess, who purchased Barbury Castle Farm and Upper Herdswick Farm, situated on top of the hill behind Barbury Castle, in order to get the land, ended up driving Mikie round Temple Farm estate one morning and the pair were convinced that the idea would work.

Goess verbally agreed to go through with the plan, so Mikie started making preliminary investigations into how he could build a suitable racehorse stables at Barbury Castle, consulting architects, experts in state-of-the-art stable design, champion trainers; men who knew the business inside out and could provide the kind of specialist experience and knowledge required to establish a professional yard not only capable of holding its own in a highly competitive industry with other larger well-established yards, but also modern and forward-thinking.

'I did my homework,' Mikie said, 'I didn't want to leave anything to chance and I obviously wanted the best facilities for the amount of money there was available. I got in touch with a guy called Andrew Clark from Bristol University, who is an expert on stable design and had worked for Sheikh Mohammed. I also got Michael Dickinson, who is very well known in racing and used to be a champion National Hunt trainer, to come down and have a look. Michael had made such a good job designing and improving other top training centres, I wanted him to see the potential of what we had at Barbury and advise me on the best way to go about building a yard capable of producing winners.'

Goess was impressed with Mikie's ambitious planning but there was still a lot of uncertainty about whether the whole thing would get off the ground. 'All the time I was consulting experts and getting them to come to Barbury to have a look at what I was planning to do, there was a doubt Conrad would actually commit himself fully to the project. We sort of had an agreement that I would actually come and train at Barbury but it was far from watertight.'

So the waves of doubt continued to crash against the fragile structure of Mikie's vision, and Goess wasn't helping. He had already expressed concern over funding, and unknown to Mikie had made plans to lease the house at Barbury Castle Farm to some of his relatives. It had been empty for some time and Mikie, who needed a place to live after deciding to leave Newmarket, had wrongly, but understandably, assumed he would move in. 'I asked Conrad if I could but he had already made arrangements with one of his relatives to rent the house. He told me I would have to find somewhere else to live,' Mikie said.

It was a major disappointment, not only because of the inconvenience but also because it fuelled the doubts in Mikie's mind that Goess was not 100 per cent behind the proposed development of Barbury Castle Farm into a racing stables where Mikie could fulfil his dream to train thoroughbred horses. If he was going to give it his best shot, Mikie really needed to live on site and yet Goess had already made his own plans. 'It was a bit of a shock because I presumed we had some kind of deal which included the lease of the house. Conrad had other plans.

'I and several of my Christian friends were praying constantly and that's when the first miracle happened. I was looking for alternative accommodation and worrying that the whole thing may fall through when I got a phone call from Conrad, saying his relatives were no longer coming to Barbury so I could go ahead and move in. It was a direct answer to prayer.'

This was the end of 1989 and Mikie moved from Newmarket to Barbury in time for Christmas. He continued to pressure Goess into finalizing the whole project and at the same time formulating plans for the design and construction of the yard. By this time he had made up his mind to build modern American-type barns instead of the traditional English type of stable. Again he went to design expert Andrew Clark, who had already designed for John Gosden and other top trainers, for advice on the construction, so as to maximize ventilation without getting draughts and combat the menace of respiratory viruses by improving the air flow and maintaining a constant temperature.

He would make enough room for 34 horses in two 17-box barns and include an isolation or quarantine area for new arrivals, as well as improving the farmhouse and building two bungalows and two flats for the staff he planned to hire. Plans to improve the road across the Marlborough Downs to Barbury Castle and work on the gallops were also in the pipeline, and despite the continued uncertainty that Goess would actually go through with it, Mikie stood firm on the count's rather tentative verbal assurance and forged ahead.

At the beginning of December 1989 he took the bull by the horns and informed potential owners that Barbury Castle Racing Stables would be up and running and ready to receive its first lot of horses within 18 months.

It was a huge gamble because Goess wasn't even sure his family trust would come up with the cash needed to fund the project. Mikie was planning to invest a large amount of his own capital in the project but he still needed the financial muscle of the Goess family trust to pull it off, and somewhere in Austria the people holding the purse strings were threatening to cut off funds. Mikie didn't know that, but bad news travels fast and it was already on its way.

'I thought everything was okay and the only thing I was really worrying about was what I was going to do while the yard was being built,' Mikie said. 'I had settled in the house, told potential owners, agents and other trainers that it was all systems go, now all I needed to find was a job to tide me over.

'I thought, "I've got to work down here, can't just sit around doing nothing," so I approached trainer Richard Hannon and said, "I was wondering if I could come and work for you," and he said, "Oh brilliant, I was just thinking I need someone to help me enter my horses in the right races." It was another answer to prayer and I ended up getting a position with Richard as an assistant trainer.

'I had actually talked to another trainer, Barry Hills, before I talked to Richard. I already knew Barry because he was one of Sheikh Mohammed's trainers but he said no, he didn't have a job for me because he already had three assistants, which is too many really, and he didn't feel it right to bring me in. But he did offer me a job managing one of his racing syndicates which I accepted.'

Hills is one of horse racing's great characters. Small and dapper, he learned his craft the hard way as jockey, stableman, form expert and gambler. He won enough money punting to try his hand at training and has never looked back.

Hills moved to the fabled training centre of Manton, high on the Downs above Marlborough, from Lambourn in the mid-80s to take over from Michael Dickinson, who had been hired by Robert Sangster to rebuild the historic but derelict yard. Hills calls Manton 'the perfect place to train good racehorses' and Mikie must have felt a slight twinge of disappointment when Hills closed the door on the opportunity for him to work there.

Above: Bruce Raymond riding Mikie's first winner, Massiba, at Windsor, 1992.

Right: High Altitude poised for take-off at Newbury, November 1996. One of Mikie's favourites, High Altitude was his 100th winner at Haydock Park in December 1997.

Above: Joking apart ... Mikie shares a smile with HRH Princess Anne during an afternoon of polo at Windsor Park, 1990.

Above: Mikie receiving the Queen's Cup at the Royal Tournament, Earl's Court, 1979.

Above: Another successful ride for Mikie at Larkhill, 1978.

Right: Marathon Man! Mikie racing in London, 1989.

Below: Lord High Admiral, out on his own and heading for victory at Sandown, May 1995.

Right: Mikie aged nine, on first pony Beaumont, with his sister Charlotte on Tony. They shared a saddle but on this occasion it's Mikie who's bareback.

Left: Outside the Heaton-Ellis family home at Chitterne, Wiltshire, 1974. From left to right: Mikie's father, Peter, his younger brother, David, Mikie, his younger sister, Charlotte, his grandmother Millicent and his mother Prudence.

Right: Mikie and his specially-adapted quad-bike on the gallops at Newmarket, 1987.

Right: Mikie and Katie's wedding day, Harlow, 1984.

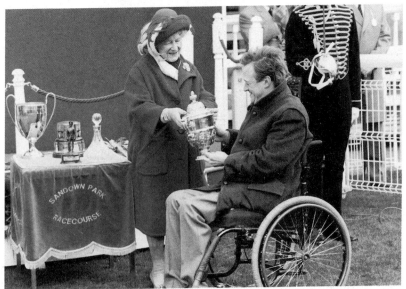

Receiving a gold cup from HRH Queen Elizabeth The Queen Mother, Sandown Park.

Above: Six times winner Mullitover at Lingfield, September 1995.

Right: Pat Eddery on Reported, winning the City of York Stakes, 1992.

Below: Mikie's horses trying out, Marlborough Downs, Barbury Castle.

Above: Building for the future. The new American-style barns at Barbury Castle Racing Stables begin to take shape.

Above: Malborough Downs 1998. Mikie training his horses near the Stables.

Hills was sixth in the leading flat trainers' table in 1997 with impressive figures of 78 races won and over £1 million in prize money. Seven years earlier, when Mikie asked him for a job, Hills was operating at the very top end of the business, training for such owners as Robert Sangster (who actually put Manton on the market in late 1989 for £15 million), the Saudi Arabian prince Khalid Abdullah and Sheikh Mohammed, and saddling the winners of almost all Europe's top events.

While overseeing developments at Barbury Castle, Mikie took on two further jobs: managing Hill's eight-horse syndicate at Manton and going to Hannon as his assistant. 'I worked every morning until late in the afternoons and nights. I had one day a week off from Richard which was the day I used to go and work with Barry and his son John, who was also training out of Lambourn, as racing manager of their big syndicate.'

Once again it was a most informative period for Michael. He learned a great deal from Hannon, a former drummer with sixties pop group The Troggs and one of the most respected trainers in the game, while enhancing his already glowing reputation as a judge of form with Barry Hills' syndicate. 'Working with Richard was a study in how to treat people and his relationship with owners. He makes racing fun but it was also hard work.'

Each morning at dawn Mikie used to get into his BMW, which Sheikh Mohammed had allowed him to keep as a parting gift, and drive from Barbury Castle through Marlborough and out to Salisbury Plain and Hannon's yard at East Eversleigh. He would quickly assemble his wheelchair before swapping it for the Honda four-wheeler, converted to hand controls, which he used to follow Hannon and his horses out of the yard.

Up on the gallops he would watch each horse intently, exchanging knowledgeable remarks with the jockeys as they rode by and also with Hannon; a man who was becoming more and more impressed with the ability of a man who couldn't walk or ride but was nevertheless making great strides towards the fulfilment of a dream that many thought was beyond his reach.

Mikie has observed many trainers and their individual methods of teaching horses to race but as far as his biggest influence is concerned it's got to be Hannon. The former pop star was on his way to the top when Mikie arrived at East Eversleigh in 1990. That year Hannon, with Mikie's help, had 80 winners including Tirol, the winner of both the English and the Irish 2000 Guineas.

That success paved the way for an even better season in 1991 and the following year Hannon became the leading trainer on the flat, although it could have been so different had fate twisted the other way during a moment of mad confusion at a busy crossroads.

That was the day Mikie nearly killed Hannon. Tirol had just won The Craven Stakes – the Guineas trial – at Newmarket and the pair were on top of the world as they headed back to East Eversleigh. As they approached a crossroads Mikie's view was partially obscured so he asked, 'Is it all right?' Hannon checked and said 'No', but Mikie thought he said 'Go' and hit the gas.

'I suddenly saw Richard ducking right down on the floor and then this other car went screaming past us. I think Richard thought it was all over.'

Maybe fate opened the right door for Mikie after all. Hannon was just the kind of guy he needed to work with before starting up on his own and it's possible that a year as assistant to Hills at Manton would not have been as beneficial.

Mikie: 'Richard was the last person I received training from and he was different from all the trainers I'd seen when I was with Sheikh Mohammed. They were the top trainers who'd got top-class expensive horses sent to them to train, which was not how I was going to start because usually a trainer just starting out gets the lower-grade horses. Richard has got a reputation of doing very well with not-so-good horses, and so watching the way he trained and the way he ran them was quite a influence.

'He has a knack of getting results from horses that are not meant to be good horses. He gives the impression of being really laid back and not caring too much, but he almost always gets it right. When I went to East Eversleigh as his assistant in 1990 we had about 160 or so horses in training, which is a lot, but Richard has a meticulous eye for detail and he knew exactly how each horse should be performing and if they were ready to run.

'He does things differently from other trainers but his methods work. I think one of the secrets of his success is that he gets a really good communication back off the horses he trains. He would watch a horse and make a decision about it which was not the obvious decision, like the horse looks as though it's lame, when it is lame, but he would say, "No, that's okay, it can run tomorrow," and the horse was okay the next day and maybe won. He would run a horse when the vet advised him against it, but he would make the right decision and the horse would run well. It's just a gift he's got.'

So Mikie continued to shuttle back and forth between Hannon's place at East Eversleigh and Manton, where he managed Hills' syndicate one day a week, at the same time pressing on with the design of Barbury Castle. In early 1991 Conrad Goess got his first look at the final blueprint. He had already vetoed one design, but then disaster really struck.

The Goess family trust said they would not go ahead with the building of Barbury Castle Racing Stables until Upper Herdswick Farm, situated on top of the hill behind Mikie's place, had been sold. It was a crushing blow because a sale seemed impossible in the current economic climate. Farms and land were just not moving. Goess's hands were tied, and Mikie suddenly realized that it would take a miracle far greater than the one which had enabled him to take over the tenancy of the farmhouse to realize his dream of training horses from his own yard.

By this time he had done an enormous amount of groundwork and potential owners were already expressing an interest in sending horses to Barbury Castle. Mikie's bold mailshot was looking more and more like a big mistake.

The news from Goess was not good. He predicted it could take years to sell Upper Herdswick. The harsh reality for Mikie was that his hopes and dreams were now in real danger of ending up like the farm on the hill; derelict and empty. 'I must admit I started to doubt,' he says, 'Conrad was not optimistic about the future because it was a bad time for farming and virtually impossible to sell land at that time. It looked as though things were not going to work out the way I hoped they would.'

So Mikie started praying again – this time for a buyer for Upper Herdswick. He had an idea, not necessarily inspired by God, but inspirational none the less. He would call his old friend Jim Old, the trainer of Dunrose who a decade earlier had carried Mikie to the very edge of his life. The big-hearted steeplechaser had long since passed away, but Old was very much alive and looking for a new place to train his racehorses. Coincidence? 'I don't think so,' Mikie said. 'I believe it was God opening another door.

'All the way through this I had had to learn how to trust on a daily basis. There was no way of planning too far ahead. God was giving me enough faith to get through each day and when it seemed like things were about to go wrong He would come through for me. I prayed for a buyer for Upper Herdswick and Jim Old's name came up.

'Someone told me he was thinking about moving from his yard at Shepton Mallet, so I called him and told him about the place up the road from me and how it would be a great place for him to train. It was an answer to prayer because he came straight up, had a look around and fell in love with the place.'

Old quickly made up his mind that he wanted to train from Upper Herdswick and brought in one of his owners, Wally Sturt, a shrewd property developer, to negotiate on his behalf with Conrad Goess. Old and Sturt were driving a hard bargain but they met their match in the Austrian count and talks reached boiling point. Mikie recalls: 'It was quite stormy and the deal was on and off.

'There were several hiccups and Conrad was very tense about the whole thing, and I remember thinking that perhaps it wasn't such a good idea. But Jim was still very keen to go through with it, and I knew that Conrad really wanted to sell the farm so that I could start training at Barbury Castle. I had my moments of doubt but I believed God would work things out and He did.'

In the spring of 1991 Sturt and Goess agreed a deal and Jim Old signed up as the new owner of Upper Herdswick. Mikie was relieved but he was not out of the woods yet. The protracted sale of Upper Herdswick had put them seriously behind schedule and there was no way Barbury Castle would be ready until the end of 1991. Mikie had told potential owners August, so he was faced with a dilemma: put his plans back 12 months and aim for the 1993 season or bring plan B into action – rent another yard and start training from there while Barbury Castle was under construction.

He chose the latter, but initial plans to rent one of the four yards at Manton fell through. Time was running out, because to be a full trainer in 1992 Mikie had to start getting horses in no later than autumn 1991. Putting his string together at Manton would have been ideal but in May that year Robert Sangster quashed the idea.

By that time Hills had moved out of Manton and relocated to Lambourn. He had failed in a bid to buy the estate from Sangster – who was at that time asking £15 million – with a view to bringing in other trainers, including Hannon, to train from the four yards. Sangster had lined up Peter Chapple-Hyam – 12th in the flat trainers' championship in 1997 – to work his string out of Manton from the end of 1991 and he wanted vacant possession.

It was always at the back of Mikie's mind to rent one of the four yards on the Manton estate from Sangster anyway; a contingency plan in the event that Barbury Castle Racing Stables never got off the ground. 'That's why Sangster's refusal to let me train there was such a raw break,' he now admits. 'Training out of Manton was my back-up plan so when Robert said no I started to get anxious about the future. It was a difficult time because I couldn't see how it was all going to work out.'

A man called Toby Balding came up with the answer, just in the nick of time. It was Balding's brother Ian who had first put Mikie on to the idea of training out of Barbury Castle and had set up that first meeting with Conrad Goess. Now it was Toby Balding's turn to help out. Mikie found out that Balding was moving his training operation to Dorset for a couple of years and was looking for someone to rent his old yard at Weyhill, near Andover. Again it was the answer to prayer.

Mikie: 'It came right out of the blue, just like Jim Old's interest in Upper Herdswick. I asked Toby if I could rent some of his boxes at Weyhill. He said, "Yes, no problem," so we thrashed out a deal so that from August 1991 I could start to put together my string of horses. But again it only just happened at the last minute and was the result of lots and lots of prayer.

'We prayed constantly through the whole period, from my introduction to Conrad right through to renting the boxes off Toby. It was touch and go some of the time but God had his hand on the whole situation. He just wanted me to trust and pray each day and He only gave me enough for one day at a time. But that's how it's got to be – one day at a time.'

True to his word Mikie started to put his string of horses together in August 1991, but his real preparation for his first season as a full trainer did not take place at Toby Balding's Weyhill yard. It took place at a Christian retreat near Basingstoke. Mikie spent one week in fellowship with other believers, reading his Bible, praying and worshipping God. It was a very important time for him: time to reflect on the events of the past year, time to look at the future, time to thank God for all that He had done.

'It was a fantastic opportunity to spiritually start me off on my venture as a trainer and since then I've always tried to have a week or several days spiritual holiday each year. For me it's a bit like Grand Prix racing, where you go in for a pit-stop to get refuelled and re-equipped to go out again into the race of life.'

6

......

Still They Ride

She remained a mystery. Outside her stable, whether in showjumping, cross-country, or dressage, Eva was the coolest, most responsive horse one could wish to ride. She rarely put a foot wrong, was always brave and never gave less than 100 per cent.

Her owner bought Eva as a yearling from a relative in Ireland for £5,000 and schooled the horse herself at a yard close to her Cheshire home. Eva was named after Evita Peron, her owner having visited Buenos Aires a year earlier and fallen in love with the horses that lived on the ranch where she stayed. She was very proud because Eva was a beautiful looking horse with her pretty face and dark bay coat, natural athleticism, and willingness to please.

But away from the arena Eva became an unpredictable creature of malicious intent. She could not be trusted. The people who looked after Eva had three rules: never turn your back on her, never share the stable with her, and never walk behind her.

As soon as she was tacked up and ready to compete or just exercise Eva was as sweet as a nut, a perfect lady. At other times, like when her bed needed changing, or she needed grooming or feeding, or the farrier or vet came to visit, Eva was transformed into half a ton of pure hate. Her show name was Ryan's Daughter – named after the man who bred her and the area where she was born, which was where they shot the film of the same name in south-west Ireland – but most people called her 'bitch'.

Once a man who didn't know Eva came to visit the yard and stood outside her stall. He was waiting for someone and Eva caught his eye. 'Come on then,' he said, 'come on.' But Eva ignored him and after several attempts to coax her to the stable door he gave up and turned away to see if he could see whoever it was he was waiting for. He had just broken rule one; fatal.

Eva made her move. Clinically and quickly. The man probably heard the clink of Eva's front shoes on the concrete floor where the shavings were brushed back to form a crescent behind the door, but nothing else. The next thing he knew he was down on the floor outside Eva's stall, clutching the back of his head and feeling a lot of pain and warm sticky blood. She had bitten him, violently hard, and her lips were still stretched back over her big yellow teeth as he staggered to his feet and walked away cursing.

Eva loved to bite and kick and there was her favourite trick: bucket throwing. She had a metal feed bucket until they realized what she was up to. Each morning they would find it outside her stall, sometimes several yards away, dented. Eva picked it up in her teeth and threw it at one of the stable girls once. Sometimes she'd miss and the bucket would bounce back off the door or wall and end up on the floor of her stall, so she would stamp on it and kick it until someone brave enough would fish it out with a brush or rake.

One night she kicked down the wall between her stall and the next stall; it was empty because none of the other owners would keep their horses next to Eva, so her owner had to pay rent on the empty stalls as well as her own. Eva broke the toes of an experienced farrier, headbutted the vet and broke someone's collarbone with her teeth. She also stamped on a dog, almost killing it, and bit the face of another horse which required surgery to close the wound.

Her distraught owner sent Eva to an equine behaviour specialist – a horse shrink – but it did no good. She even tried herbal medicine, hypnosis and faith healing without any luck. Eva's split personality could not be tamed. Hers was one of the most disturbing cases the horse psychiatrist had ever seen, and yet Eva kept winning. As soon as she saw her bridle and saddle she became a completely different horse.

In that respect she was very predictable, and the fact that she was utterly trustworthy outside her stall saved her from being 'given to the gypsies', a frequent threat from a very frustrated owner. Eva was incredibly successful at eventing, so good in fact that her owner was frequently offered large sums of money by people who had been bowled over by her sheer class. Little did they know.

Depending on your response to such extreme behaviour she was either the most gifted or the most horrid of horses. I was one of the believers in her wonderful athleticism, intelligence and responsiveness, and yet everything changed when she returned to her stall.

Eventually, after winning hundreds of first prizes, Eva was sold. Her owner wanted a horse her daughter could ride and look after without worrying about getting bitten or kicked or hit by flying buckets. The owner explained, with a rather poignant analogy, 'I have just replaced Eric Cantona with Gary Lineker because I know Gary will behave himself on and off the field. Eric is a brilliant player, but he can't be trusted and neither could Eva.'

Ironically, her new horse was unpredictable as a performer. During one point-to-point race he galloped out of control off the track and into the car park and in another just stopped and refused to move for twenty minutes.

So much for the theory of biddability. Horses are supposed to be clever. What sets them apart from the cow or the sheep is the size of their brain. It is significantly larger, especially the neocortex, the part responsible for learning, so the main attraction of the horse as a working animal is its ability to understand and obey. If only man knew precisely what goes on in that expanded organ between those two twitching ears.

As Peter Scudamore once remarked to a reporter as he trudged back to the weighing room following his awful experience on Tarconey at Cheltenham in January 1989: 'Don't ask me what happened, ask the bloody horse.' Tarconey had ducked out at full gallop and crashed into the wing of the final fence when the race was in his grasp. And who can forget Walter Swinburn's terrible accident in Hong Kong in February 1996 after the two-year-old he was riding veered diagonally across the track after leaving the starting stalls, before shooting off in the opposite direction and crashing into the running rail.

Some racehorses just can't be trusted, although I doubt any horse could be as bad as Eva. I heard about a fine Irish thoroughbred, a top horse for a National Hunt trainer a few years ago, who was moody and would refuse to eat and had a habit of turning her back on the stable lads and staring at the wall when it was time to turn out, occasionally biting and kicking when the mood took her. A friend of mine owned an ex-steeplechaser, a big old grey mare, who wouldn't come out if it was raining and used to stamp and kick around if he wore yellow, and there is a wonderful story of a top middle-distance racehorse who wouldn't settle in its box unless accompanied by a sheep.

Weird and wonderful but part and parcel of the task facing any horse trainer. Horses are individuals, like people, and each one is blessed – or cursed – with emotional and mental traits that either make a trainer jump for joy or swear in sheer anger and frustration, although generally the horses you find at professional racing stables are finely tuned and balanced creatures who can be trusted on and off the track.

There are exceptions to the rule, though, and Mikie has had his fair share of difficult and unpredictable horses. In fact most of his best horses have had slight quirks. Ironically, Eva's new owner was a Christian who prayed regularly for the horses in her care, and, believe it or not, the horse's behaviour improved greatly, although I hear she is still very unpredictable.

Mikie admits to occasionally praying for a sick horse, and there were one or two horses at Barbury Castle during the writing of this book that he warned me to watch out for during guided tours of his two barns. I don't know why but some horses will just go for you. Fortunately most of the horses at Mikie's yard are brilliant with people and he has some real characters in training.

Take Irish-bred Artful Dane, a great favourite of Mikie's and a horse who is lucky to be alive, let alone racing. He has an impressive record and had just finished second in a race at Goodwood as a three-year-old in 1993. He was in transit on the M27 heading for Royal Ascot when he became unsettled in the horsebox, kicking his way out of the narrow groom's door while the vehicle was doing 30 miles per hour and jumping on to the motorway. Artful Dane then cantered down the M27 on the right side, with cars overtaking him on the inside, nearly jumped the barrier into the opposite carriageway and ended up stopping to eat grass. 'We wondered if he'd survive,' Mikie said. 'The vet was up all night sorting him out. He suffered terrible cuts and fetched a lot of skin and muscle off forcing himself through a door only half his size, but all the damage missed the vital parts and I got him back on the racecourse at the end of that year, although he didn't run particularly well.'

It was down to Mikie's skill as a trainer that Artful Dane was racing at all that day. At the end of his three-year-old year something was stopping him from reaching his full potential in races. Mikie, who is skilled at watching these fine creatures, noticed that Artful Dane carried his head up quite high, and although he or the jockeys who rode the horse never heard him making any noise or having problems with his breathing, both symptoms of respiratory problems, Mikie had a gut feeling there was something wrong.

So he sent Artful Dane to an equine hospital in Bristol where they taught him to canter on a treadmill and then endoscoped him, looking down his throat while he was cantering, and discovered that when he was getting tired his airway wasn't working properly. Surgery cured the problem, and Artful Dane went on to win a big race thanks to Mikie's ability to understand the silent communication of horses. They talk to him in sign language and more often than not he understands, although not always.

Reported, a fine, powerful mover, tried to tell Mikie something was wrong before an injury ended his career. He arrived at Barbury Castle as a three-year-old, which is considered quite old when you are buying a racehorse, and ended up winning the City of York Stakes with Pat Eddery as his jockey, technically the best race that Mikie has won. 'He was a machine. To see him moving on the gallops in the morning was a great sight. He was an absolute dream to watch and train, he'd float over the ground.'

But one day Reported started acting strangely. He would get really worked up when he went out on the gallops, playing up and refusing to train properly. It was completely out of character, but a few weeks later Mikie found out why.

Reported suffered a stress fracture of a small bone in his leg. 'He knew it was coming,' Mikie told me. 'When he was getting worked up he was talking to me, telling me that he didn't want to train because of this potential problem. Had I rested him then maybe he would not have suffered the fracture. Fortunately it wasn't bad enough to have him put down but it effectively ended his career.'

Mikie had a similar experience with another horse called Petra Star. She had a lot of potential but every time she came to the beginning of the canters she would suddenly stop, refusing to go down the hill. Mikie suspected something was wrong and sent her for X-rays which revealed flaky bones in her knees. 'She was in pain, and playing up every time she got to the top of the canter was her way of telling me she was in pain.'

It may sound obvious, but it's not. Training horses to race is a complex business and is as old as racing itself, although it has grown in sophistication and complexity during the past 25 years or so as never before. Once upon a time, long before Mikie even saw his first horse, trainers were severe to the point of cruelty, using methods such as 'sweating' which involved horses being galloped long distances clad in blankets to make them lose weight quickly. These days, thankfully, trainers like Mikie favour a kinder, more gradual programme to prepare horses for the racecourse and keep them fit and well.

Training is more of a science than an art, but it's an imprecise science and trial and error and gut instinct must be resorted to. No two trainers follow exactly the same formula and no two horses respond in exactly the same way. Fast work over sprint distances may bring one horse to race fitness while another of similar breeding and conformation will require a more patient approach, perhaps involving half-speed work on an uphill gallop, to achieve a similar state of readiness.

For a trainer, the ability to produce fancied runners 'ready to the minute' is the ultimate goal and a skill that will always receive the highest praise, but just how such perfection is reached will vary from one yard to another. In today's commercially orientated horse-racing industry it is no longer enough for a trainer to understand horses alone. They must be multi-talented to cover all areas of a business that is a 365-day-a-year occupation, involving long hours, a high burn-out rate and complete dedication. But a genuine love of horses and an eye for a good horse are essential, and a trainer who cannot understand horses is no trainer at all.

So the job involves a little science, some common sense, a bit of luck and the ability to communicate with another species that has its own unique language. This natural affinity between trainer and horse is a gift that people like Mikie are born with. It's much more than simply having an eye for a horse, it's about understanding and instinct. That is how a trainer can tell the difference between a horse simply being mischievous or just feeling down and a horse with a genuine problem.

Mikie watches and learns and gets inside the horse's head. He has to be able to know them as individuals to understand what makes each one tick. Horses have souls, they feel emotion. They have good days and bad days, highs and lows, and each one in its own way communicates these feelings to the people around it. Of course, their primary function is to win races and they are first and foremost highly tuned athletes, which is why there is no hint of over-sentimentality at racing stables like Barbury Castle. The horses have a job to do and it's the job of the trainer to make sure they do it to the best of their ability.

Mikie's basic philosophy is: 'I've got a stable full of athletes that I'm getting fit for a race but I've got to teach them to be racehorses.'

Horses are not born racehorses and a trainer is only as good as the horses he is training. It's a simple equation that adds up either to success or failure. The more winners a trainer has, the more chance he has of winning the best races, and the more of those he wins the more chance he has of training the best horses. It's an upward spiral, but there is a lot of luck involved and no matter how good a trainer is he cannot control fate.

Mikie: 'Horses change so much between the age of one and three and no matter how well you do your job it's impossible to predict how a horse will turn out. There is a great deal of luck involved in the process of buying a young horse and teaching it how to race. In between the time you buy a yearling at the sales and its first race a lot can go wrong. You don't always know what character you are getting. You don't know what's going on inside its head, whether they have a big heart or some defect in their basic emotional, mental, or physical make-up.

'I've got to determine whether they are sprinters, middle distance or long distance. I've got to find out about their character and how best to train them, and it's all a matter of communication, two-way communication. By watching them every day I should be able to see how they are, their general well-being. They speak to me with their behaviour, movement and performance.

'For example, when they come out of their boxes I know how they normally behave, whether they are jumping out or whether they come out slowly, that's all part of their character. I also use science to help me, taking lots of blood tests, taking temperatures in the morning, checking how much they are eating, keeping an eye on their weight. It's all part of the overall picture, seeing how they are on a daily basis and getting them ready for a race.'

The normal practice is to buy horses when they are yearlings – 18 months old – at the sales for the owners, who pay around £12,000 a year to keep a horse in training. It's a high price to pay, especially when the chances of making a profit from winnings are quite slim. If Mikie gets a horse that is not cut out for the job he is quick to tell the owner. 'It would be dishonest to keep a horse on that I know is not good enough,' he says. 'Some trainers do but I don't. I like to think that my owners trust me to do an honest job with the money they pay me to train their horses. It would be easy to keep taking their money even if their horse is useless, but that would go against my Christian beliefs.'

It's pretty rare that Mikie ends up with a dud because he always does his homework, using a process of elimination that although not foolproof is quite reliable. He always works with a bloodstock agent, who will look at every horse at the sales and draw up a list of 20 or 30 horses for each day of the sale that he knows are more or less a safe bet. Mikie: 'These are the horses the agent knows I will like, which saves me the time of looking at useless horses. I want to spend as much time here at the yard training the horses and as little time at the sales as I can.

'So I fly in on the day of the sales and look at the horses the agent has picked out. What I am looking for is basically an athlete. Is it fit enough to be an athlete? I get an indication from their attitude; temperament. A horse has to battle at the end of a race when he gets tired for no reason. The horse doesn't know that first past the post gets the glory. They have got to have a resolute character.'

The buying of horses, like the breeding and training of them, is an infuriatingly indefinite discipline. Highly respected and highly paid experts have been known to advise their clients to part with huge sums for yearlings who proved use-less as racehorses, while the fortunate few have purchased champions very cheaply. The bloodstock business, like the training business, is uncompromising and ruthless, and is certainly no place for the novice. Hours of careful research will have been undertaken by highly qualified experts to identify the top prospects in terms of breeding and conformation. The charting of pedigrees goes back many generations and bloodstock agents will go to endless trouble before attempting to assess the merit of an offspring, and only when armed with every available detail will bids be made.

Having the pedigree in front of you on the sales catalogue page helps because the majority of good horses are well bred, and according to the pedigree, or bloodline, a trainer can see what he is buying; the breeding reveals whether the horse is meant to be a sprinter, middle distance, or long distance. If you look at a horse that is bred to be a sprinter and it's a long-legged horse that has the appearance of a 'stayer' – possessing natural stamina – or if you've got a 'stayer' that has the appearance of a short, power-packed sprinter, it's a sign there could be something wrong, although there are exceptions to every rule.

Lord High Admiral, a Canadian-bred bay gelding and one of Mikie's best loved and most successful horses, was bred as a miler and ran over a mile and a quarter for a previous trainer, but Mikie discovered he had great natural speed and dropped him back to a shorter distance. The horse had never won a race over distance but now he's won 10 races as a sprinter, although he remains a very difficult horse to train. At the age of 10 Lord High Admiral is one of the oldest horses at Barbury Castle and commands enormous respect, but he can be extremely infuriating.

Mikie: 'He is a horrible horse to train. He's got two speeds, slow and fast, and there are times when he just refuses to go. But he's a great old character and everyone loves him.'

It's quite unusual for a sprinter to retain its speed as long as the age of 10, but Lord High Admiral is one of those exceptions to the rule that make horse racing so unpredictable. He has terrible knees and has already had two operations, forcing Mikie to train him on the hills instead of the gallops. 'He could go on for another year or two,' Mikie says, 'but I doubt he'll get any easier to train. I've only got two people who can ride him because he is so difficult. My assistant Clive Cox, who is a brilliant rider, gets on with him really well but it can be a nightmare working with a horse that's got so many little quirks.'

Artful Dane, when he's not jumping out on the M27, is also a bit of a pain to train. For a start, he hates being in front in a race and has a lazy streak which makes him a difficult horse to ride. Hard work makes him bad-tempered so Mikie has to resort to a little kidology to get him fit; cantering on the hills instead of working the gallops tricks Artful Dane into thinking he's not doing too much hard work while in reality he is.

It's not the first time and it certainly won't be the last time Mikie has had to hoodwink one of his horses. The story of Speedy Classic, a nine-year-old top sprinter, illustrates very well the fine line between science and sheer cunning and the way Mikie likes to train.

Bred in the United States, Speedy Classic, a beautiful-looking brown horse, came to Barbury Castle via Mikie's former employer Barry Hills, who said the horse was 'f— useless' and couldn't wait to see the back of it. 'Speedy Classic was really awful when I first got him,' Mikie admits. 'He was a nightmare and in one of his first races for me he went straight off the track and through the rails on one side. I was beginning to wonder if Barry was right, but I knew he had ability because he galloped quite well in trial gallops and I just felt he had potential. It was a gut feeling.'

After watching him for a while, Mikie came to the conclusion that Speedy Classic was being held back by a medical problem. 'The overall impression that I got about the horse was that he was unhappy because he was in pain. It was impossible to say for certain, but I was sure something was hurting him; it was just a feeling I got.'

Mikie called in the vet and following a preliminary examination which drew a blank, Speedy Classic was endoscoped, which revealed bleeding in his lungs caused by broken blood vessels, a very painful condition that gets worse during exercise. Mikie was proved right and the problem was successfully treated with powdered snake poison, which is a pro-coagulant.

However, in his next race Speedy Classic faded badly at the end. The problem now was purely psychological. The horse didn't know he was cured. Mikie: 'I couldn't tell him that he was okay but somehow I had to show him that he was cured and he could now go out and run without hurting. I had to let him know that the pain wasn't going to return.'

So Mikie 'put blinkers on' and cotton wool in his ears to make him feel completely different during a race. It was a cunning move because Speedy Classic, despite being cured by the snake poison, could remember the time when running caused him pain, so when he galloped he'd just think, 'Ah, this thing all over again,' and stop.

The blinkers and cotton wool took his mind off the bad memories and made him feel he was doing something different. 'It was enough to get him through the psychological barrier that had been stopping him. The blinkers and cotton wool kind of blocked things out and made him feel better, happier in himself. The first time we tried it he came in third at Lingfield and he suddenly realized he was okay. I'd got the message through to him and his character changed. The horse that Barry thought was useless looked really happy for the first time and started winning. He's been very successful for me ever since – winning 13 races and even having a race named after him.'

Still They Ride

Two other great examples of Mikie's ability to spot potential and succeed with horses who have physical problems are Golden Melody and Massiba.

Golden Melody is a little bay filly who was sent to Barbury Castle home-bred. She has a lovely character, but if you look at her straight on when she's standing in her box, you notice that her legs are completely crooked, pointing out in every direction. 'You would never buy a horse with legs like that,' Mikie told me, but he was determined to make a good racehorse of her because he had a gut feeling she had potential.

Mikie: 'Yes, I felt she could be a decent horse, so I trained her very carefully up the hills and taught her how to jump. She was a useless jumper but we schooled and schooled her, and she got better and better until she won her first start over hurdles. It was very satisfying to see a horse like Golden Melody come good, but I always felt she could do it – she's not a great performer, but she has a big heart.'

The filly called Massiba, Mikie's very first winner, was lame and spent a lot of time training on a water treadmill at Lambourn. They couldn't ride her because her legs were lame and it took a few visits to Lambourn before she was fit enough to train and eventually race. The days spent walking on the water treadmill kept Massiba physically and mentally fit until she was cured of lameness, and seeing her win at Windsor races was a real triumph for Mikie. 'It was a fantastic feeling,' he said.

But Mikie doesn't always go to such lengths to get a winner. Some horses, like the unusually named Arterxerxes, a five-year-old bay gelding, are relatively problem-free and are a joy to train. Arterxerxes is not the world's best horse, but he tries his heart out and has a lovely genuine character. Mikie rarely gets sentimental about the horses he trains but he's got a soft spot for Arterxerxes.

Mikie: 'He's got a big honest head and a big honest eye and is a lovely horse to train. You can read him like a book, because when he is out on the gallops he is jig-jogging and happy and pulling at his rider and if he's not right he is quiet, so I can see at a glance if he is right or wrong. He is what I call a proper horse.'

But even 'proper' horses worry, that's why routine is vital. Sudden change makes them anxious, that's why some horses die when they stop racing – because they can't cope with the sudden change.

Mikie makes sure his horses are turned out and ridden and fed on time at the same time each day. This meticulous time-keeping makes horses feel secure, because they have an unsettled life early on which can breed anxiety and uncertainty. In many cases they are raised as foals somewhere and moved to another stud where their mother has been covered by another stallion, before returning to their home stud. At 18 months old they are separated from their mothers and sent to the sales, and they end up being broken at a strange yard before training to become racehorses.

Mikie: 'They don't know whether they are coming or going during the first two years of their lives. That is why getting them settled into a routine is so important. The young horses like to train in the same place every day, but the older they get the more bored they get training in the same place. Some horses worry even when they are in a routine. Some need to be turned out into the paddock in the afternoon to stop them getting stressed out, and others need to feel secure with the person who looks after them each day. Sometimes when a horse isn't doing very well you change the person who looks after it, and you just find the new person has a better rapport with the horse and it's happy again.'

Trainers break racehorses like any other horse: introducing the bridle and the long rein, then leaning someone across its back, and eventually riding it for the first time and teaching it to be a racehorse. Mikie: 'It's very satisfying to buy a young horse that has never been ridden and break it in and teach it how to race. It's a long process but the end result, when the horse matures and wins its first race, is worth all the hard work.'

Finding out if a horse is mature enough to start serious training is easier said than done. You can have two virtually identical two-year-olds and one will be ready to race while the other won't start until the following year. Very often the best horses take longer to mature and those bred for steeplechasing, which requires great stamina, tend to mature less quickly than sprinters.

Gauging emotional maturity is something of a lottery but Mikie uses a tried and tested scientific method to check for physical maturity. It's a simple process of taking an X-ray of the horse's knees and checking for bone growth. The vital cartilage doesn't show up but the growth plates of bone do, and the closer they are together the more mature the horse is. It is a good guide to the skeletal maturity of a horse and reveals what even the most highly trained naked eye cannot see.

Mikie X-rayed four two-year-olds' knees before the start of the 1998 flat season. They all looked ready to go but only one of them passed the X-ray test. The others were too physically immature to train and race. Bringing them on too soon can cause a lot of damage, sometimes enough to end the career of a budding young racehorse before it's begun.

Mikie puts his trust in medicine and science and his own knack of understanding horses, and he also relies heavily on his riders. 'It's vital to have good riders,' he says. 'A good rider will tell me so much about a horse when he's been out on the gallops or the hills with it. This feedback about the horses' behaviour and movement is essential to my job. Even if I could ride I would still rely heavily on my riders, because they are the ones who ride out every day and get to know the horses. It's two-way communication again: between the riders and me and me and horses. Teamwork really. We rely on the horses to run well to keep the business going and they rely on us to look after them and make sure they are happy.'

Mikie started with just six horses, which he trained from Toby Balding's yard. There was only one really good horse among those and that was a filly called Santana Lady, who won several races. The number increased to around 20 when Mikie started training from Barbury Castle in 1991 and stayed at between 25 and 30 for a couple of years, until Mikie had 45 on his books in 1994. That figure dropped during the next two years after a virus went through the yard but increased to 33 the following year. In 1998 Mikie had 37 horses in training at Barbury Castle, which is over-capacity for his two 17-box American barns but may actually increase next year, if he has a successful flat season this time.

Compared to the horses owned by high flyers such as Martin Stoute, John Gosden, Henry Cecil and John Dunlop – the top flat trainers in 1997 – those at Barbury Castle are mediocre. Stoute's horses won 84 races, earning over £2 million in prize money during the 1997 flat season. Mikie's horses achieved only a small fraction of that. The gulf between the top and bottom of the flat trainers' table is vast and the fact that most horses never win a race of any sort is a sobering truth.

The pyramid-like structure of the Pattern – the overall design of racing established 28 years ago to group the best horses of each age and sex over various distances – is designed to give less talented horses the chance of winning races at their own standard. For many seasons the only official group of races was that of the five Classics, the five most important races of the year and restricted to three-year-olds: the two Guineas races over a mile at Newmarket in the late spring, the Derby and the Oaks over a mile and a half at Epsom in the summer and the St Leger over a mile and three quarters at Doncaster in the autumn.

In 1965 the Jockey Club set up a committee to investigate the pattern of racing, with the intention of providing a balanced programme of high-class, non-handicap races for horses of all ages and over all distances throughout the season. A system was devised to select races which would be included in four categories: Groups I, II and III and Listed races.

Pattern races include the five Classics, and Group I, II and III and Listed races are followed by handicaps and maidens, for horses who have not raced before. In general terms the Classics and races in Group I can be regarded as of championship-level importance; those in Group II are just below top level and those in Group III are stepping stones to higher things.

It is every trainer's and owner's ambition to own a horse who is the best of his calibre and capable of winning at Group I level. Mikie's ultimate ambition as a trainer would be to have a winner in the Derby, but that may never happen. Reported's success in a Listed race at York is Mikie's best effort so far but fortunes can change quickly in racing. There are plenty of examples of horses who have improved at such a rate as to take everyone by surprise, and thus there is considerable incentive to keep trying to advance a horse up the ladder.

The bottom line, though, is the old maxim that a trainer is only as good as the horses he trains, and more often than not it takes a stroke of luck to enable a trainer of Mikie's status to join the likes of Stoute, Gosden, Cecil and Dunlop at the top of the flat trainers' ladder. In footballing terms Mikie is currently in the Second Division of the Football League; Stoute, Gosden, Cecil and Dunlop are the Manchester

Uniteds and Arsenals of flat racing's Premiership. Mikie would need to win quite a few important races to get promoted. Even then further success would very much depend on having enough money in the yard to buy better quality horses to maintain good performances at the highest level.

Arsenal could not hope to win the Premiership or the FA Cup with a team of Second Division players and Mikie is unlikely to win Group I races with horses who can just about hold their own in Listed races. 'To move up into the same league as Michael Stoute,' he says, 'I would need to win several decent races to attract owners who can afford to pay upwards of £100,000 on a horse.

'Sometimes an average trainer can get lucky and win a few top races with an average horse and get really noticed, but it's a bit of a vicious circle really. To win a Group race you need a quality horse, but most of the owners with enough money to buy quality horses capable of winning the top races go with trainers with a record of winning the top races. So it can be difficult to move up the ladder, although it's not impossible.'

Reported may have had the potential to go all the way for Mikie. He cost £100,000, a record for Barbury Castle, but injury ended his career and Mikie admits: 'It was a big disappointment for me at the time. I think he could have gone on to win bigger and better races than the City of York Stakes, but that's the way it goes in racing sometimes.'

The brightest prospects at Barbury Castle at the time of writing are The Gene Genie, a three-year-old English-bred bay colt, and Northern Spring, a two-year-old chestnut colt. Northern Spring cost 48,000 guineas as a yearling, a fraction of the cost of the yearlings out of top studs like Camas and Kilcarn which can realize upwards of 900,000 guineas.

Mikie has gone against racing tradition by revealing the identity of the horses he believes could make his best winners.

Trainers are very superstitious about this and believe that naming their up-and-coming stars is tempting fate, in other words the curse of injury.

'I'm not bound by superstition,' he says, 'I believe in hard work and honesty and God. It's a very tough business and extremely precarious. A 48,000-guinea horse would go out with the washing at a top yard but with a good team behind me and faith in God, owners continue to send their horses for me to train. And hopefully we'll keep going and have more success in the future, although to a certain extent our future lies in the ability of the horses.

'It's a well-used saying but you really are only as good as the horses you are training, and that is the bottom line in this business.'

7

......

Tell It All

In the early days, when Mikie first started training at Barbury Castle, he was approached by an agent representing a very rich man who made his living selling pornography. He is one of the wealthiest men in this country and loves horse racing, and he wanted Mikie to train two of his many horses. It put Mikie in a very difficult position, because he wasn't sure if it was right for a Christian to work for a man who's made all his money out of pornography. He certainly needed the business, because owners are hard to come by, but still Mikie felt uneasy and told the agent, 'I'll think about it and get back to you.'

Mikie read his Bible and prayed for guidance and asked Christian friends for advice. The mother of his close friend Ralph Crathorn said: 'I think it would be wrong to judge this man, and refusing to take his business would be the same as saying you are better than he is just because you are a Christian. And if you looked in the lives of some of your clients you would probably discover other immoral things, so you should not refuse to train his horses.'

Another friend said: 'If you are not willing to associate with people of the world who do things that go against your Christian beliefs, then how can you ever share your faith? You should meet this man and tell him about God.'

'They were right but I didn't think I was big enough for that job,' Mikie said. 'I thought, "No, I'm not doing that," and virtually made up my mind to call the guy's agent and say, "Thanks, but no thanks." A few days later I went to church in Marlborough and the sermon was about the power of Jesus and how we can do all things through him. It made me realize that it didn't matter that I lacked the confidence to tell someone about my faith because God would give me the strength to do it. It's not through our own strength or power, but by God's Holy Spirit, that we can do all things in Him.'

During the service an amazing thing happened. One of the ministry team said: 'There is someone here who is suffering with a pain down his right arm. Please come forward so we can pray for you.'

It was Mikie. In his haste to get to the church on time he had pulled a muscle getting his wheelchair out of the car, and by the end of the service his right arm was quite painful. So he went forward for prayer. But to his surprise the person who was ministering to him said: 'You are worrying about something and don't know what to do. God wants you to stop worrying and go ahead and do the thing that you feel you can't do.'

Mikie called the agent and took the two horses owned by the pornography tycoon, but they were both useless as racehorses and were put up for sale. Before they were sold the owner sent his business partner to Barbury Castle to talk to Mikie about the potential deals on offer. He arrived on a Sunday and, after discussing the sale of the two useless horses, he and Mikie went to a wine bar in Marlborough for lunch.

'I didn't want to be there because I like to keep Sunday special, but I wanted these horses off my hands and had no choice,' Mikie said.

The 'porn king's' partner was a bit of a shady character and Mikie felt slightly uneasy. It was the weekend of the rugby home internationals, and being a rugby fan Mikie chatted about the previous day's games. The other man also liked rugby and told Mikie, 'I've played a bit of rugby at the hotel where I've been staying.'

The conversation changed from rugby to horse racing and back to rugby again and the other man kept mentioning 'hotels' and spending a lot of time away. Mikie was curious and asked, 'What hotel are you talking about?'

He didn't realize that 'hotel' is inmate slang for prison. The man smiled: 'Ford Open,' he said. 'I've just done three years in Ford Open for selling illegal pornography.'

Mikie was surprised, but he was even more surprised when the man said, 'I've got to ask you something. Why are you always smiling and so happy all the time when you are in a wheelchair?'

It was the moment Mikie had worried about; time to share his faith, although not with the 'porn king' but his partner instead. 'It's Jesus,' Mikie said, and told the man all about the love of Christ and the Gospel message and how God had changed his life and made him a better person and how, despite his injuries, he was fulfilled and happy as he had never been before.

The other man listened and when Mikie had finished admitted, 'I knew there was something special about you.' He had seen the sunshine in Mikie's life, and for a moment it had illuminated even the darkest corners of his own life. God had transformed Mikie's moral dilemma into a wonderful meeting of two completely different souls and the chance to share his faith.

But the story doesn't end there. Several years ago I worked as a football writer for a newspaper owned by the 'porn king' and my daughter kept her pony at a yard owned by a man who was a close friend of his. Coincidence? Maybe, but in 1996, before I even knew Mikie, a friend of mine, who is a racing journalist on a national paper, told me a great story about an ex-con who worked for the 'porn king' but mended his ways after hearing the Gospel message.

The story, in which we'll call the ex-con Mr X, went something like this:

> I went to see the 'porn king' to check out a lead for a story about him building a stud in Hampshire. I had been tipped off by a source at the football club that the 'porn king' owns and my paper wanted to know if it was true. It wasn't, but I picked up an even better story as I waited to see the 'porn king'. Mr X, who I knew used to be the 'porn king's' business partner, pulled up in his Mercedes and said, 'Oi, come 'ere, I've got a scoop for you.' Mr X told me he and a very famous footballer were planning to buy a top racehorse for a lot of money. The story actually checked out but the 'porn king' later insisted, 'Don't believe a word Mr X says, he's been acting strange for months. Last month he told me he couldn't work in the porn business any more because God is watching him. Ha, ha, ha . . . what a plonker.'

There are some Christians who might say Mikie's decision to train the 'porn king's' horses was nothing more than a cop-out, but anyone who knows Mikie knows he is the last person to compromise his faith. He is not afraid to put his business and career on the line to honour God, no matter how great the risk involved.

Once he was asked to stop one of his horses winning a race by crooked owners who wanted to make a fast buck. It may seem inexplicable that the owner or trainer of a horse in a race might not want to win it; yet there are many reasons why a horse might be given an easy race to the extent of avoiding victory. Most innocent of these is that he may not be fully fit, and may 'need the run' in order to get more tuned up – if he can win he will but he will not be put under too much pressure. More devious is the practice of deliberately having a horse lose – 'stopping him' or 'hooking him up' with the full consent of owner and trainer.

The reason for doing this is so that the horse's handicap mark does not get too high and 'friends' of the owners or trainer can plan to make a good deal – 'land a touch' – from backing the horse in a future race. The theory is that a horse that is not winning will be given a lighter weight than the handicapper, or a few modest runs when not trying to win – 'not off' – will make a horse appear worse than he is and he will then start at longer odds when he is 'off' or trying to win.

The idea of the handicap was introduced to give lesser horses a chance of winning races, although some owners and trainers hate the practice. In a handicap the weights to be carried by individual horses are adjusted, with better horses carrying more than the less good, so that in theory their chances are equalized. Using another footballing analogy, it's like making Manchester United players wear lead boots against Manchester City.

According to Luca Cumani, the Newmarket trainer, 'Handicaps are a form of Communism. Ideally, the best horse should always win a race, and handicaps are a denial of that principle. Handicaps make up half of the races run in England but the only people that really love them are bookmakers. They want them because they offer the biggest profit.'

It's a fair and common criticism that handicaps are not a true representation of what racing should be about because owners and trainers are governed by another person's opinion of their horse. Once they find a horse is overrated there is a huge incentive to cheat.

Mikie was asked to cheat, but he refused and it almost cost him a good horse. 'I could easily have gone along with it and got away with it,' he said. 'It's not uncommon in racing and I know many ways to stop a horse from winning. But there was no way I was going to do it even if it meant falling out with the owners, which I knew would probably happen.'

The horse in question is one of Mikie's most successful, but at the time it was out of form and its owners were getting itchy. 'Don't worry,' Mikie told them, 'he will come back into form,' and a few weeks later, true to his word, the horse started to perform well on the gallops and was entered for a race.

Four people had equal shares in the horse and one of them called Mikie. 'Shall we have a big bet on him?' he asked, but Mikie wasn't sure the horse would win and said, 'I think it could go either way, so I'm not going to back him.'

'In that case,' said the owner, 'don't let him win. We want you to stop him. Don't let him win!'

There are many ways to stop a horse: drug him, overwork him, overfeed him or bribe the jockey. Mikie did nothing and the horse came in first at 20–1. The owners were furious and called Mikie. One of them said, 'We are going to take our horse away and send him to another trainer, or we might sell him. We are really angry with you because you let him win when we told you not to.'

So Mikie said, 'I'm not going to cheat for anyone but I like the horse and don't want to lose him. Let me buy him off you.'

Two of the owners didn't want Mikie to have the horse, but one did and in the end they reached a compromise. Mikie agreed to let them off the previous month's fee, approximately £1,700, in return for the horse. Ten days after buying the horse it ran in a race and won. The prize money was just under £2,000 and Mikie sold the horse immediately for the same money as he had paid for him. 'Once again God honoured me for being honest,' he said. 'It would have been easy for me to go along with the owners to keep them happy, but it was more important for me to do what God wanted me to do in that situation and in the end He made sure I didn't lose out.'

Mikie could once have lost out big-time when he chose to go to a Christian meeting instead of taking his most important owner to the races. Fred Sainsbury, a local farmer who struck it rich when he discovered gravel under his land, owns five of the 37 horses currently in training at Barbury Castle, including the Irish-bred geldings Absolutely Equiname and High Altitude.

Sainsbury used to own more horses, but even so the income from having five in training is in excess of £60,000 a year, which makes him vital to Barbury Castle's financial viability. A few years ago Sainsbury's horses at Barbury Castle numbered eight or nine, and he also bought Mikie a car and horsebox, so you can see how important he was to the yard.

In October 1996 Mikie ran one of Sainsbury's horses in a race, but couldn't go because he had to go to the sales in Ireland instead. Sainsbury was quoted as saying, 'If another one of my horses runs and Mikie doesn't go I'm going to take all my horses away.'

It was very important to Sainsbury that the trainer of his horses should accompany him to the races and he felt very strongly about it, enough to carry out his threat. Their relationship was going through a bit of a sticky patch anyway, mainly because the Barbury Castle horses didn't have much luck during the 1996 season, but in early 1997 Mikie risked losing Sainsbury's business completely.

He was scheduled to attend a Christian meeting in Marlborough on the same day that Absolutely Equiname was running in a race at Haydock. It was the only day that Mikie could run Sainsbury's horse but he was determined to go to the Christian meeting instead. He couldn't even get his assistant Clive Cox to accompany Sainsbury to Haydock because Cox's brother was getting married the same day.

The Christian meeting happened only once a year and was vital to the planning of church services in the Marlborough area. It had been arranged months in advance and was the only day that everyone could make.

Mikie told his secretary Judith Balding, 'I'm not going to Haydock with Fred Sainsbury because I'm committed to this Christian meeting, and I feel that is what God is asking me to do.'

Judith was shocked: 'I think you are making a mistake,' she warned. 'You know how important Mr Sainsbury is, and don't you remember what he said about taking all his horses away if you didn't go racing with him again?'

Mikie's Jewish friend Derek Gold, who is also an owner, said more or less the same thing. 'I know your faith is very important to you but your relationship with your owners is also very important, and I think you should go to the races with Mr Sainsbury instead of attending your Christian meeting.'

Even Fred Sainsbury's housekeeper Sally feared the consequences if Mikie went ahead with his plan. 'He'll freak out and take all his horses away,' she said.

Losing eight horses would cost almost £100,000 a year and that kind of loss can severely damage a young yard. Mikie was worried and with everyone bombarding him with warnings, he didn't know what to do for the best, although in his heart of hearts he believed he should go to the Christian meeting.

As well as praying about the whole situation with a prayer partner, Mikie sought the advice of close friend and fellow Christian Graham Daniels, manager of Cambridge City football club. Daniels said, 'Going to the race will not make any difference to how the horse runs so you should go to your

Christian meeting, because it's important that you trust in God and be led by the Holy Spirit.'

Mikie was still in two minds, but then God spoke to him through the testimony of a Christian girl who was speaking at a meeting at Marlborough College. She was going through a difficult time in her life, but said that God was leading her through the dark and although she could not see where she was going she was to trust in Him and be led.

'The message hit home,' Mikie said. 'It went straight into my heart and was the answer I had been seeking. I was going to trust God and be led by Him through this difficult situation, even though most people were telling me that I would probably pay a heavy price for going to the meeting.'

Mikie phoned Fred Sainsbury and said, 'I need to talk to you, can I come over to see you?' Sainsbury said yes but was quite surprised. So early one winter afternoon, on the eve of Absolutely Equiname's race at Haydock, Mikie went to see Sainsbury and said, 'Look Fred, I've got to tell you something that's really bothering me. You are an important owner of mine and if you tell me I've got to go racing tomorrow then I will, but to be honest I've arranged to go to a Christian meeting and I really think I should go there instead of with you to Haydock.'

Sainsbury looked at Mikie, who expected the worst. Sainsbury rarely backed down and had already told people that he expected Mikie to watch Absolutely Equiname race at Haydock. But he smiled and said, 'I think you'd probably be better off at church.'

'I was flabbergasted,' Mikie recalls. 'We went into the house to have a cup of tea and you should have seen the look on the face of Sally his housekeeper. She could not believe that he'd said that. I think we both expected him to blow up.'

Judith Balding drove Sainsbury to Haydock the following day and she couldn't believe how calm he was. He didn't even mention Mikie or the Christian meeting or his threat to take his horses away. Absolutely Equiname won easily and Sainsbury was very happy. Later that evening Mikie saw Judith at a charity ball at Newbury racecourse and she said, 'There must be a God, it's incredible how it's all worked out.'

In 1996 Mikie was faced with another dilemma: Sunday racing. The previous year he had been actively campaigning to keep Sunday special, but the industry was pressing hard to race on both days at the weekend and it was inevitable that horses would eventually run on the Sabbath. They did for the first time in 1996.

Mikie: 'I was doing nothing about it and it was heading quite close. What woke me up was people kept asking for my opinion because they knew I was a Christian and I didn't want it to happen. They motivated me and I started actively campaigning against Sunday racing.'

He wrote a letter to *The Times*, which Henry Cecil co-signed because he didn't particularly want to see the racing week extended, on behalf of the people who worked at Barbury Castle and all the other head lads, stable-lads, stable-girls, work riders and anyone else involved in the day-to-day running of a racehorse yard in England.

Mikie: 'I was fighting Sunday racing under the banner of all those people who deserved at least one day off a week. Up until 1996 when the law was changed, they only had one full day off and that was Sunday. In my letter I said Sunday is meant to be a family day.

'One of the arguments was that they had an easy day on Monday because there is no racing on that day. That sounds all right in theory but the fact is, though, on Monday children go to school, and if they are married their partners are probably working somewhere else, so it's not a family day. I put the best case forward I could to keep Sunday special without getting into all the stuff about God and why the Sabbath should be kept as a day of rest. That happened later.'

As a guest of Emma Freud on BBC Radio One, Mikie found himself on the opposite side of the debating table to Labour MP Robin Cook, now Foreign Secretary, a keen horse racing fan and an advocate of Sunday racing. They were arguing about the pros and cons of racing on Sunday when Mikie took the opportunity to share his faith. Cook just shut up and listened. The same thing happened on Radio Five when Mikie and Lee Richardson, PR man for the Jockey Club, had a debate live on air with people phoning in to give their views on the subject, although in the end Mikie, and everyone else who opposed Sunday racing, lost out to the majority.

During the first season of Sunday racing in 1996, Mikie made a rather hypocritical error of judgement when he advised one of his owners to race their horse on a Sunday. 'It was a really good race for the horse, so without thinking I told the owners it was an opportunity not to be missed. She did run in it and finished third, but I should never have suggested it after all the fuss I made trying to stop Sunday racing – and they were quite willing to run in another race on the Monday. I was wrong.'

It may be pure coincidence, but no sooner had Mikie declared the horse to run on the Sunday than he broke his hip after turning over his Honda four-wheeler on the gallops. 'I had a big rethink after that,' he says. 'Even though I had been totally against Sunday racing, I don't think I really believed it was in their best interests to stop my horses running in races I knew were right for them to run in. Part of the skill of training horses is putting them in the right race, and if the right race for them is on a Sunday then probably they should run.

'The way I handle it now is quite simply, I never suggest to an owner that we should run on a Sunday, but if they want to then I say OK, we'll do it. So it's not my decision and I am never at the course on Sunday. It's a bit of a compromise but I'll never push for a horse to run on a Sunday, even if I know they probably should run.

'I entered a horse for a Sunday race by mistake once, because I just looked through the race book and saw a date for a race which was right for the horse without realizing it was on a Sunday. I had already told the owner by the time I found out what I'd done so my hands were tied. I nearly went last year because an owner wanted me to go, but I got a puncture on the way so I never got to the track. Maybe it was God's way of telling me not to compromise.'

Quite often, as a Christian, you've only got to compromise your faith once to permanently taint your testimony. It's a sad truth that many people who profess to live their lives according to the teachings of the Bible are quick to judge. I hate to admit it, because Christians are ridiculed enough as it is, but when I started to research this book the reaction from some Christians was so bigoted that I couldn't quite believe what I was hearing. One church leader said, 'A Christian racehorse trainer! There's no such thing. A genuine Christian could not work in an industry that is fuelled by gambling.'

It is one of the most ridiculous things I have ever heard. Bigots, dogmatists, call them what you will; they wouldn't recognize the truth if it materialized in the form of an eighteen-pound sledgehammer and hit 'em right between the eyes.

Gambling is rife among trainers and can lead to dishonesty, but Mikie is neither a gambling man nor dishonest, and the fact that he earns a living from an industry largely funded by gambling doesn't make him a hypocrite. Gambling, for which horse racing is heavily criticized by Christians, is a very unimportant motivation for him, although because he had quite a substantial bet on one of his own horses in a selling race at Leicester in the spring of 1997 some people accused him of being two-faced. 'They never believed me afterwards,' he admitted, 'but in my defence there is much more to the story than meets the eye. It may have looked like I had a bet on a horse but it wasn't a gamble, it was purely a calculated financial move.'

The racing papers didn't see it like that. They reported that Christian trainer Michael Heaton-Ellis had 'had it off' and a coup had been landed. The real truth behind the headline was that Mikie made a business decision to run a horse called Brave Envoy in a low-grade race to boost the horse's confidence and establish his market value.

He had a bet on the horse to win at 16–1 to cover the cost of buying it back afterwards. In a selling race half the money from the sale of a horse goes to the racecourse and half to the owner. The bidding for Brave Envoy started at £3,000 but in the end Mikie had to buy him back for £10,500, and even with his winnings still ended up £1,700 out of pocket.

If you want to be pedantic about it, Mikie gambled and I guess he paid a price. He's lost the trust of some Christians, who believe he compromised his beliefs because it suited him to have a flutter which he later disguised as a straightforward financial move. 'I don't really care what people think. I know why I did it and I know that I'm not a gambler.

'I don't like to see people throwing their money away on backing horses. My own personal view of gambling is that it's simply not being a good steward of the money we have, but there is no instruction in the Bible about gambling and the only difference between trying to make money on stocks and shares and backing a horse is the odds.

'In the industry as a whole a lot of prize money is funded by gambling and as a trainer involved in the sport I am providing a medium for people to bet on. I train horses to race and one of the main reasons for horse racing is to bet on the outcome, so I have ask myself: is it right for a Christian to be involved in this process?

'When you go to the races and see the bookies with their wads of cash taking money off people, when you take a good hard look at this sleazy side of the business, it's got a horrible feel to it. But Jesus would have been right in there with them, showing them a better way and telling them about salvation. That's why I believe it is right for me to stay in an industry that is funded by gambling. God wants Christian men and women in every walk of life. The Bible teaches us that Jesus didn't cut himself off from the world, did he? No, he went out and mixed with all kinds of people.

'He was a light to the world, even in the darkest places, and people criticized him. They said, "You can't go talking to prostitutes, you can't be seen in such and such a place, you can't be involved with those undesirable members of society, those who drink and gamble and blaspheme." Jesus did not judge and neither should we. Life is not perfect, people are not perfect, even Christians. But God's love covers a multitude of sins.'

8

·······

As a Flower Blossoms

What is the greatest pain a man can feel? What is his greatest fear? John T. Lewis, the legendary Texan stuntman, once remarked: 'I've broken and smashed my body a hundred times and stared death in the face a whole lot more, but the greatest pain I've ever known is the pain of a broken heart and the greatest fear is the fear of losing the one I love the most.'

Lewis, a former jockey, died in a riding accident six months after becoming a Christian, but at his funeral this new-found hope was overshadowed by the presence of his three ex-wives and two long-term girlfriends, who spent the entire service scowling at each other. Lewis's brother, the late Bobby T. Lewis the horse trainer, remarked, 'I bet John's looking down from heaven with a pretty girl angel on each arm. Lord forgive him, he just can't help it.'

And neither can Mikie. He has a weakness for the opposite sex. He just can't help it. Ironically, being a Christian probably makes things worse. Girls are attracted to a man of God, especially a good-looking man of God who trains racehorses and mixes with the rich and famous.

He has even admitted to me that a good chat-up line is: 'Would you like to come to church with me?' This doesn't make him a bad guy or hypocrite and it certainly doesn't undermine or devalue his Christian testimony. It's just the truth, and the truth is strong and good and can only lead to freedom, emotionally and spiritually. The hypocrites are those who pretend they don't have a problem or weakness or flirt with pretty girls.

There is nothing wrong with sexual attraction. It's okay to be a Christian and enjoy being in the company of members of the opposite sex. It's okay to take pleasure from noticing a good-looking, sexually attractive person. But sometimes it's not, especially when you or other people get hurt or it becomes a problem. Mikie's weakness has almost got him into trouble several times. He has been guilty of cheating and womanizing and even now he finds it incredibly difficult to resist temptation.

It's a standing joke among those members of the press who know Mikie. 'Always surrounded by the prettiest girls at the race track, trainer and Christian Michael Heaton-Ellis.'

During the past few years the national press, especially the tabloid newspapers, have received frequent tip-offs about so-called romantic liaisons between Mikie and various 'pretty girls'. Some of them were close to the mark but most were miles out, just the figment of someone else's overactive imagination, paparazzi or society poppers jumping to conclusions for a fast buck – horse trainer dances the night away with TV star in Barbados; chats up millionaire businesswoman at dinner party; shacks up with pop star – distortions of the truth.

'Yes, he's a bit of a babe magnet,' one of Mikie's old friends told me. 'Whenever I've seen him at the track he's chatting up some nice-looking girl. I don't think he can help himself, although he's a good, honest guy, not the sort who uses people or cheats.'

Not any more, anyway. God has changed Mikie, made him a better person. Less selfish, less sexist, less racist, less of a show-off. But once upon a time, before his marriage, Michael Heaton-Ellis would not think twice about being unfaithful. He was a Casanova until the accident took away his ability to fully consummate a relationship, and even that didn't stop him from chasing girls and women.

He has frequently been seen at fashionable London nightclubs with a pretty girl sitting intimately on his knee, and even during the writing of this book he was involved in some kind of relationship with a pretty German princess who moved close to Mikie's home after falling out with her royal family.

He admits: 'It is a problem for me, or should I say a weakness. It always has been, and even now as a committed Christian I have to pray every day for strength to avoid temptation. It's one major area where I get attacked. I'm sure the Devil knows that I find women hard to resist, because I find myself in all sorts of crazy situations where it would be easy for me to give into temptation.

'I used to sleep around and cheat on my girlfriends. I never betrayed my wife Katie, but for some reason I seem to attract women and since I've been a Christian it's happened even more. After Katie left me I became a Christian and when we met some time later she said, "You are more attractive as a man. There's sunshine that wasn't there before."

'That light in Christians is very attractive, so that's why the *Daily Mail* writer Nigel Dempster coined the phrase: "Michael Heaton-Ellis, born-again Christian, always surrounded by the most beautiful women at the race track." And that is something that has always happened to me, and it's always tempting to get involved. You have to be very strong to resist the urge.'

There is a line in the chapter about Mikie's Christian faith in the Christians in Sport book *Winning is Not Enough* that says, 'The broken-hearted girlfriends he left behind were not ditched selfishly or carelessly.' It makes me laugh every time I read it, because Mikie was very good at letting them down lightly. A true Casanova rarely extinguishes the fire. He just lets the flame die out but keeps the embers burning.

Several times since his accident Mikie has flirted with disaster as a result of his weakness. Once he got involved with a young American girl half his age and ended up embarrassed and cheated and hurt. It happened in September 1987, only a few weeks after his wife Katie had ended their marriage.

'I went to the races one day at Yarmouth and saw this really beautiful girl,' he explained. 'I thought, there's a lucky jockey or owner somewhere because she can't be on her own, and I didn't think any more about it. But when I went to Newbury races a few days later she was there again. I noticed she was smoking, so I said to a friend I was with, "Go and ask her for a light and find out who she is and if she is with anybody."

'Finally she came back and said, "Well, she's a girl over from America and she doesn't know many people, but she likes racing and is having a look at different racecourses." I thought right, that's it and wheeled over and started talking to her, and ended up taking her out to dinner. We did not spend the night together but stayed in the same house as one of my friends, Kim Bailey, one of the top National Hunt trainers, and the next day she came with me to see the horses at Barry Hills' big yard at Manton.

'We then had a few drinks at lunchtime and she told me this story: "I was at the races in America and I called home to ask for a lift. My mum and dad and brother came to pick me up but were killed in a car accident on the way to the track. I was devastated and ran away to England to start a new life. I need somewhere to live and a job, what can I do?"

'I immediately started to back off and thought, "Oh no, I'm in a bad situation here," but I was attracted to her and decided to help her find a job. I found her a place to stay at a friend's house until she found a job and a place of her own. While she was staying there she had quite a lot to drink one night and passed out. My friend became quite suspicious of her and went through her bags and found a letter which she had written to her parents.

'It said: "Dear Mum and Dad, I've left home not because I don't love you but for another reason. I just had to leave. I am in England but I am okay so don't come looking for me."

'The next day my friend confronted her and she admitted that she had been lying. I honestly thought she was about twenty-two or twenty-three years old but she was actually only fifteen. My friend called her family and eventually her brother came over and took her back to America.

'I was embarrassed, cheated and hurt, because my ego had been inflated and suddenly I was left looking very stupid after being duped totally by a fifteen-year-old girl. Being with her had given me a boost to my pride after my wife decided she did not want me; this beautiful girl with me at the races and all my friends saying, "Wow, who's that girl with Mikie? Lucky so and so." People were knocked out by her looks.'

He was lucky he found out when he did. The press were on to the story, and the fact that Mikie had at that time one of the most enviable and powerful jobs in horse racing as Sheikh Mohammed's racing manager would have made great headlines. The Sun newspaper were sniffing around, but for some reason Mikie was spared the embarrassment of reading about his fling with an American schoolgirl in England's biggest-selling tabloid.

He was not so fortunate when the *Daily Mail* decided to run a story about his relationship with Princess Diana's cousin Frances Roche. This was two years after his wife Katie O'Sullivan had left and because they had made the marital home at Newmarket larger by extending it, Mikie decided it would be good to have lodgers to help pay the bills. He took in Frances Roche and another person.

He explained: 'It just happened that I ended up with Frances as a lodger. It wasn't planned. But a few weeks later someone rang me from the *Daily Mail* and said, "Is that Michael Heaton-Ellis?" And I said, "Yes," and she said, "We hear that you are going to start training racehorses," and I said, "Yes, it's fantastic, brilliant, I've got this great new place down on the Marlborough Downs with fantastic gallops and it's going to be tremendous . . ." But I could hear on the end of the line this girl going, "Yeah, yeah," and she wasn't interested in that at all, and then she said, "There's just a couple of other things I want to ask you. What's happened to your wife?"

'I said, "Well, we're separated, we are getting a divorce and she's living in Lambourn and London." She said, "Is it true that Frances Roche is living with you?" I said, "No, she's not living with me, she's a lodger in my house. She's paying rent to stay in one of the spare rooms. So no, we are not living together." The journalist then said, "Is she your girlfriend?" "No, she's not," I said and she said, "Okay, that's fine, nice to have a chat with you," and put the phone down. What I didn't realize was that the *Daily Mail* had got a photograph of Frances and myself and decided that we were an item.'

The idea that romance was in the air sparked two days before the telephone conversation with the *Daily Mail* journalist, when Mikie was dancing with Frances Roche at Annabelle's nightclub in London. When Mikie does a slow dance in his wheelchair, the girl sits on his knee. The paparazzi must have thought Christmas had come early, because there was Princess Diana's first cousin sitting on the knee of a top racehorse trainer, with her arm round his neck and a huge smile on her face.

'It was all quite romantic really,' Mikie admitted. 'They say there is no smoke without fire, but there wasn't a lot of fire in it. Two days after the phone call there's a big headline in the *Daily Mail* and a picture of Frances and myself saying: "She's only the lodger!" – exclamation mark. The truth is, Frances wasn't my girlfriend but we were becoming quite close. She had a steady boyfriend but there was definitely something between us, although it never came to anything.'

In Mikie's kitchen at his impressive country house at Barbury Castle Racing Stables is a photograph of a beautiful girl with amazing eyes and a sexy smile. I don't know her name, and Mikie never really wanted to talk about her, but she is a Christian and they shared a close friendship until she said, 'I don't think this is right,' and walked out of his life. He keeps the photograph, though, and smiles every time he sees her smiling face. Memories.

Temptation happens to us all – but for some reason Mikie is enticed more often than most. Without wanting to sound like some preacher from the old-time gospel hour, the Devil likes nothing better than to put temptation in the way of a Christian, and Mikie admits: 'I do believe that some of my experiences are designed to test my faith.

'I believe that there is a Devil and that there is opposition to God as well, and sometimes when I have been used in any way by God I've got a backlash when something bad happens, and it usually involves a woman. I'm not blaming the Devil for my weakness for women but there are times when I swear the Devil has set a trap for me.'

On his way home from London, where he had visited an exhibition of work by the Christian artist Charlie Mackesey and talked to a TV producer about the possibility of a bio-graphical film, Michael saw a young girl who works at the kennels close to his racing stables. He stopped his car and she said, 'Hi Mikie, I'm really upset about my horse, can I talk to you about it?' So she got in the car and said, 'Oh, it's really sad. I don't know whether I'll be able to keep my horse, because the girl who owns it with me wants to sell it and I can't afford to look after it myself.'

Mikie was just about to offer his advice when suddenly she jumped straight on top of him and started kissing him passionately.

'What happened?' I asked. 'Nothing, because I realized it was wrong. I just know that was the Devil's way of trying to make me fall because he knows that's my weakness, and if I'd been a non-Christian something bad would have happened.'

That is not such a terrible admission, because at least Mikie is honest and strong enough to resist temptation because of his Christian faith. You may laugh at the idea that the Devil devises these evil plans to try to trip Mikie up, but some of the situations he has found himself in stink of devilish collusion.

A friend, whose wife owns several horses, called him to a meeting in London and said to Mikie, 'I've got a girlfriend and don't love my wife any more, but I know she's really attracted to you so do you fancy taking her off my hands? She fancies you like mad and I won't mind if you want to start a relationship with her.'

Mikie was shocked and told his friend, 'I can't do that because we are both friends, and even though your wife is a lovely person I am a Christian and wouldn't even consider it.'

Mikie was tempted by the offer of a relationship with another married woman whom he met at a dance. She just came right out with it and said, 'I really feel attracted to you, can we just have a really good time? We can meet and sex would be nice, if you want to, or we could just get together and enjoy each other's company.' Mikie replied, 'No, you're married,' but now admits: 'It wouldn't have taken much for me to have slipped. She was very attractive, really beautiful, and you could see guys just knocked out by her looks every time she got up and danced. I was very tempted, but there would have been a price to pay. Someone would have ended up getting hurt and God would not have wanted it to happen anyway.'

Mikie has been hurt very badly, more than most of us will ever know. First he suffers a fate that many would describe as worse than death, and then he contracts a terminal illness which will eventually destroy his entire person, unless a miracle happens. How desperately cruel, how terribly, terribly unlucky. And yet, his physical anguish and pain is nothing compared to that which he experienced during and after the break-up of his marriage to Katie. 'It is the worst thing that has ever happened to me, and that's saying a lot when you are paralysed and have a terminal illness.

'I loved her desperately, and deep inside could not bear the thought of losing her. It hurt me, badly, although perhaps not as much as it should. My heart was broken but I was quite hard and callous towards women, so I think a lot of the pain I felt came from anger really. It was a terrible time, though.'

The start of the love affair between Mikie Heaton-Ellis and Katie O'Sullivan could have come straight from the pages of a movie script:

Handsome army officer confined to wheelchair following tragic riding accident meets and falls in love with beautiful Irish painter. Against all the odds they climb the mountain that his injury represents. She believes love will conquer all and he struggles down the aisle on crutches at their wedding; the start of a wonderful romantic crusade with the faithful bride determined to get her brave love back on his feet. They honeymoon in some exotic location where he shares his dream of owning his own racing stables and maybe someday even riding again, and she whispers of the power of true love. They move into a quaint English country cottage and live their dream, happily ever after.

In reality the marriage was doomed from the start and it broke Mikie's heart. It would still be broken today had it not been for the emotional healing that took place in his life after he became a Christian. What really hurt was Katie's confession that she knew immediately that it would not work. The sexual problems they faced were enormous, and Mikie was realizing that the healing that was going on was emotional and mental and not physical. That was no comfort to Katie, who told Mikie if she didn't leave she would be tempted to have an affair.

It cut him right to the deepest part of his soul and in August 1987 she left.

That was before Mikie became a Christian. When Katie walked out he could have been forgiven for screaming right in the face of the whole world, tearing his heart out and crushing it until every last drop of love spilled out and she was no more than a bad memory that he would cut from his mind with all the cold ruthlessness of a director cutting a bad scene from a movie.

In reality his anger was perhaps misplaced. Sure, he didn't want to lose someone who became his soulmate for a short while, but the real reason for his rage was the inconvenience of it all. 'How dare she leave me on my own with no one to help me and no one to talk to,' he thought, summing up his rather selfish view of marriage.

Even so, the marriage break-up left him shattered, although he had enough anger in him to hit out at God. In one wrathful phone call to his father Mikie raged, 'If God thinks this is going to make me turn to Him, He's wrong.' Michael knew

God was there and he was sick of the unfair game He was playing with him.

His larger-than-life ego had been splattered in the emotional equivalent of a bad car crash and although desertion by the woman he loved had left him crippled inside, Mikie was determined to pick up the pieces and move on.

In a painfully honest interview almost ten years to the day that Katie left, Mikie admitted: 'The breakdown of my marriage came as a surprise to me because I was not paying any attention to Katie. I was selfish and too wrapped up in my life to notice she had become so unhappy.

'One day she went to see a friend in London who she said was unhappy. When she came back I asked how her friend was and she told me, "Actually, Mikie, I am the one who is unhappy and I don't know what to do. I might have to go away for a little while." Her mother came to stay but nothing was going to make it better. She left for good and there was nothing I could do to get her back.

'I wanted to make the marriage work but she'd had enough. Katie came back to see me after I became a Christian. We had a weekend together which I believed was a trial to see if we could work things out. I don't think Katie saw it like that and it didn't work. I asked her, "Do you think I've changed?" And she said, "Yes, I can see something that wasn't there before. There is a sunshine in your life."

'I knew that was God, but it wasn't enough to make her come back. I think I actually lost her a long time before she left. I just didn't see it coming, and looking back I'm not sure whether I really deeply loved her. I don't know and I question that I know what love is really.

'Years later I gave her a lift to the races. It was good to see her but we were strangers, time had slipped between us and it was like talking to someone who I didn't really know. I see her family every now and again when I go to the horse sales in Ireland. She's had a bit of a bad time. She got remarried but that ended in divorce and then she moved in with National Hunt jockey Jamie Osbourne.'

I asked Mikie if he ever thought about trying again with Katie, but I could tell by the look in his eye that there is no place for her in his new life. Another woman, maybe, but not Katie O'Sullivan. 'If the right girl came along and she was a Christian like me then maybe I'd get married again. But if they are right in what they say about motor neurone disease that could put me off. I don't want to put someone else through it.

'But I do think I have a lot more to offer as a husband now than I did when Katie and I got married. God has changed me and made me a better man. I made mistakes with Katie which I wouldn't do now. I think I'm much more prepared to listen to others, to understand and appreciate their needs.

'The Bible has taught me a lot about how we should treat each other, especially people who we care deeply about. We can learn a lot about ourselves and others from the word of God. It is the most important book ever written and Jesus is the best example today of how we should live our lives.'

Those who knew Mikie well before God changed him recall a man who was not always honest, sometimes prejudiced and always striving to get his own way, often at the expense of others. Immediately following his accident he refused treatment from an Asian doctor and would not allow a black orderly to touch him. That was Mikie's dark side emerging, although David Heaton-Ellis revealed: 'Mikie was not really with it for a couple of months after his accident. He was out of his mind really and didn't know what he was saying.'

Mikie's self-analysis: 'On the face of it I was an honest and good guy who wanted the best for himself and lived his life accordingly. I was self-seeking but there is no real malice in me. I lose my temper and I have to guard my tongue, because I am reasonably quick-witted and can be cutting. I get annoyed when I can't get my own way and in the past I've cheated and been devious to get what I want. I've lied and committed fraud and even got other people to lie for me. Before I became a Christian the only thought I had was "Can I get away with it?" I didn't care whether it was right or wrong.

'I would chance things and wouldn't be honest about the way I lived my life or conducted my business, not as I am now. I now believe it is right to be totally a hundred per cent honest, because I know that God is watching. So whatever I do I know I'm not going to get away with anything. That's not a threat, I do it because I believe it's right. There are instances in my life as a racehorse trainer where I could be dishonest to make more money but I don't and I'm proud of that. In the Bible it says look on everything that is good and righteous and do accordingly. God has made me an honest, upright man and I thank Him for that.'

Mikie has changed, and this wonderful story of a stunning blonde called Francesca says it all really, illustrating perfectly how his priorities have shifted.

This beautiful woman strolled into the racing stables one day because she wanted to buy a racehorse. She was a friend of Mikie's brother David, a professional polo player and self-confessed ladies' man.

Francesca told Mikie she was recently divorced and wanted to fill a big gap in her life with the excitement of owning a racehorse. They had an enjoyable morning together, looking at horses and chatting about life in general. She said that as soon as her divorce settlement was through she would definitely buy a racehorse and let Mikie train it.

He was as happy as a sandboy, because for a trainer of race-horses there is only one thing better than a new client – a beautiful, sexy, blonde new client.

He invited her out to dinner at the Dorchester Hotel in London and they had a wonderful evening. She couldn't wait to get involved in horse racing and not only that, she couldn't wait to get to know Mikie better. Francesca had developed a soft spot for the man who was going to help her fill the void in her new life.

The old Michael Heaton-Ellis would have been champing at the bit by this time, eager to ignite the flames of a potential romance. But not any more. Of course Mikie was knocked out by her beauty and was thoroughly enjoying being in the company of such a fine woman, but what he wasn't going to do was exploit the situation for his own selfish desire.

She had the looks and the money and the want to service his financial and emotional needs, but instead of leading her further down the road to becoming one of his clients Mikie told her about his faith instead. He recalls: 'I told her how I had recognized a huge gap in my life a few years before, and that Jesus had now filled it and given me that fulfilment and peace that only He can give.

'Her eyes immediately lit up and I knew that God had spoken through me to her. I took her to church the next week and she loved it. The love of God really touched her, and eventually she became a Christian and married a really nice guy who is also a Christian. She is now happy and fulfilled as she had never been.'

Some time later, on his return from a holiday in Barbados, Mikie found a letter waiting for him from Francesca. It said: 'I just want to thank you for the part you played in me becoming a Christian. I am so happy and fulfilled and no longer have that deep emptiness inside me, and I no longer need the excitement of owning a racehorse. I hope you understand.'

'I did, and I thought it was wonderful. I lost a potential client and, believe me, they are few and far between. But I knew I had done the right thing, and miraculously God honoured what I had done because the following week another new client came my way.'

9
....

Into the Great Wide Open

While the sun burned high in the blue Texas sky, I waited for him. I waited for hours, until the shimmering heat of the black-top highway cooled and the motel lights lit along the strip towards downtown Fort Worth, where Tom McPherson broke his back riding a bull called Wild Cherry in the American Fall of 1974.

He was late, very late, but it didn't really matter to me, because I would have waited all day and all night to see McPherson jump out of his Ford pickup and stride across the parking lot like John Wayne. I wanted to see this tough-looking, leather-skinned 48-year-old Texan rodeo cowboy walk, because once upon a time his legs were as useless as Mikie's are now. I was waiting to meet a walking miracle and I wasn't disappointed.

Of course this was a long time before I ever met Mikie, but I want to tell you McPherson's remarkable story, because there is a vital link between what happened to him between 1974 and 1995 and what happened to Mikie between 1981 and the time of writing this book in the winter and spring of 1998.

In the summer of 1994 I was in Texas to research true stories for a book called *Miracles Can Happen*. I had heard all about Tom McPherson through another professional rodeo

133

cowboy I met by chance during a flight from St Paul, Minneapolis to Dallas two years earlier. McPherson was a cripple, paralysed when a ton of prime Amarillo bull jumped on his prostrate body, until he was dramatically healed near the summit of the Hill of Apparitions above the small Croatian town of Medjugorje in the summer of 1989. It's the place where six children claimed to have seen a heavenly vision in June 1981. McPherson is just one of twelve million people from all over the world who have visited Medjugorje in search of miracles.

The damage Wild Cherry inflicted on McPherson was so severe that doctors at the nearest hospital confused him with another patient, who was rushed into casualty about the same time after falling 300 feet out of a helicopter on to a concrete runway. McPherson's torso was so twisted that the rodeo paramedics didn't know whether he was facing up or down in the sawdust.

'I became a cripple who hated life until the Lord healed me,' McPherson told me. 'It was incredible. God just kinda reached down and took all my pain away.'

I also met a man called Joseph Spears who was born blind in both eyes, and had never seen until McPherson led him to the 'miracle town' of Medjugorje in the spring of 1994. Spears was completely healed and he told me: 'I knew Tom before he was healed; afterwards I returned to my own faith because I believed God had performed a great miracle. I mean, at first I couldn't see what had happened but people kept telling me how straight his back was, and how he was running around all over the place and riding again.'

But there is no happy ending to this story. In January 1997 Tom McPherson was killed in a car crash. He was returning home from church one night and hit a concrete post after swerving to avoid another vehicle. It happened half a mile from the rodeo where he broke his back riding Wild Cherry.

McPherson had the same vision as Mikie. He wanted to tell the world about the love and healing power of God and he did until his life ended so tragically. A rodeo rider crippled in a freak accident but miraculously healed, only to wind up dead in a car wreck. And a jockey crippled in a freak accident but touched by God, only to wind up apparently dying from an incurable illness.

This is the harsh reality and cruel injustice of life, and in comparing the plight of the late Tom McPherson and Mikie Heaton-Ellis a sobering truth is revealed: even the most devout, God-fearing people are not safe when fate lashes out.

McPherson remained in the rodeo industry after his accident and returned to riding following his dramatic healing on the Hill of Apparitions, but he was planning to quit and 'work for God' full time before his tragic death. I don't really believe in omens, but when Mikie suddenly revealed to me the week before Christmas 1997 that he was thinking about quitting horse racing at the end of 1998 to make himself available for full-time Christian ministry, my mind raced back to recall McPherson's revelation that God had called him to 'preach the gospel' and not ride bulls or work as an agent for other rodeo cowboys.

Mikie Heaton-Ellis is a shining example of the difference God can make in a person's life. This remarkable man with laugh lines around his eyes radiates genuine compassion. He cares about people but he is not a soft touch. Mikie Heaton-Ellis is brave and tough and has a durable, uncompromising spirit. He is also brutally honest and a realist who accepts that his life may never work out the way he hopes it will. He believes with all his heart and soul that God is in control, but admits that His spiritual blueprint may be completely different from his own mortal plans.

Where is the Winning Post?

'Grains of sand and blades of grass, but each is numbered by God like every hair on my head and each beat of my human heart,' McPherson told me as he gazed at the stars in the big Texan sky, a million heavenly eyes watching us as we leaned against the hood of his Ford in that Fort Worth parking lot all those years ago. He had a faith as strong as the bulls he used to ride, but even a walking miracle like Tom McPherson could not hope to know the mind of God. Some days this modern-day cowboy would walk for hours into the great wide-open ranch country, seeking the will of the Maker and learning how to trust.

The land where Mikie trains horses to race is a vast ocean of rolling hills and fields as far as the eye can see. Men and horses are reduced to the size of ants in this giant landscape. It is God's country, glorious and awe-inspiring. McPherson would have been right at home.

When you come over the rise that hides the long valley sweeping majestically in front of Barbury Castle Racing Stables, it's like discovering paradise, especially in the summer when the grass sparkles like the surface of an ocean.

It is dramatically switchback, though, but with over four miles of gallops the choice is limitless. The Old Ring Gallop was used by the famous steeplechaser Brown Jack, and below the Old Ring is the new Valley Gallop, a ten-furlong stretch, and next to that a seven-furlong all-weather with three shallow bends. There is a ten-furlong winter canter and in the valley next door, the mile-long Old Valley gallop. In the opposite direction are two more gallops – the Old Sharp Ridge Valley over six furlongs and the New Sharp Ridge Hill, a stiff incline created for flat horses and by repetition for stamina horses.

Mikie has lost count of the number of times he has followed horses out into this great wide open space to watch them work the hills and the gallops. He used to ride out with them on his Honda four-wheeler converted to hand controls, but now because his arms are weak he drives out in his Subaru. His love affair with this beautiful land that became his home the best part of a decade ago is never-ending. Mikie loves the land as much as the horses that brought him here in the first place, and that is why it would break his heart to leave.

On a cold, wet Saturday morning in March 1998, when the wind raged in violent gusts and the track across the Marlborough Downs was deep in water, Mikie sat in the front seat of his mud-splattered car parked at the top of a three-furlong gallop and talked about the possibility of quitting horse racing because of his illness.

I listened and watched his face as he watched his horses, one group on the slopes of a distant hill and another ready to turn and race back up the gallop they had just walked down.

Every so often he would look through a pair of binoculars at the three horses and riders working the slopes of the distant hill, before switching his sight to the five horses and their riders down below us at the foot of the gallop. 'I love it out here,' he said. 'It's a great place to live and work but I don't know whether I'll be here this time next year. I'm not sure what the future holds for me as a trainer. God willing I could become a champion trainer, or a preacher, or both, but then again I could end up dead sooner rather than later.'

He smiled and laughed and looked at his horses again. The five nearest to us had turned at the foot of the gallop and were heading back up. Bedevilled, a three-year-old chestnut colt, led with a pair close behind; a four-year-old black gelding called Wild Sky, fitting for a morning like this, and Third Cousin, a three-year-old bay colt. The fourth, The Gene Genie, same age, colour and sex, cruised by effortlessly before the eldest of the group, a nine-year-old bay gelding steeplechaser called High Altitude, came past.

Mikie smiled again. He was pleased, especially with the performance of Bedevilled and The Gene Genie. They looked in great shape and would be ready for the start of the flat season only three weeks away.

Mikie has a way with horses; a gift. He knows how to get the best out of them and they respond to his methods, but strangely he has no deep emotional attachment to these fine creatures. He loves their athleticism and makes a living from their sweat, but after High Altitude had disappeared with the rest of the group over the top of the hill Mikie admitted: 'I don't love horses in a soft, sentimental way and there are times when I don't even like them. It's just a job to me and I think that maybe God has other plans for me, although I don't know His mind and maybe things will work out differently than I imagine they will.

'But I do feel that God is weaning me off horse racing. I don't enjoy it like I used to. Of course I still get a high from having a winner, but it's temporary. It's only a high, not a deep joy. The ultimate goal for a horse trainer is winning and that is what I enjoy the most. It gives me a great buzz but it doesn't last long. You have a winner in the afternoon and the buzz lasts until the following morning when you read about your horse in the newspapers. But then it's gone. The deep joy that comes from knowing God lasts forever, nothing can compare to that.

'It's possible I may be heading to a place where I hope to be working full-time for God, but it's all in God's timing, not mine, so you have to take each day as it comes. God can always change my plans and it's possible that I may be able to combine speaking and training.

'My illness has been a major factor in persuading me to consider quitting, but even if I get dramatically healed, which is possible with God, I still have a feeling deep inside that this business may have run its course. There have been times since I was told I have motor neurone disease I have felt like stopping, but there is still a part of me that loves horse racing and several people have told me that I should carry on.'

Barbury Castle Racing Stables is a beautiful place, nestled in a valley on the edge of the Marlborough Downs. In many ways it is an ideal existence. I know people who would give anything to enjoy this kind of life.

Mikie's lease on Barbury Castle Racing Stables expires in the year 2000. He moved here in 1991 and had it in mind to train for nine years and then maybe stop, perhaps moving into another area of the business, or simply retiring if he had made enough money. Motor neurone disease has accelerated the process, but there are other reasons.

'In my heart of hearts I don't think I am a whiz-kid trainer. I've done quite well, although I think I haven't reached my full potential. I know I am a good trainer but not a great trainer. I've been training for eight years and I've had enough success to stay in business, but if I'd been a genius I would have some real success.

'I think undoubtedly you become a better trainer as you get more experience and you can tell by looking at horses quicker what's going on, but I don't feel that my ambition is there like it used to be. Also this yard is not particularly good for having healthy horses. I suspect we might be in a bit of a natural bowl, where the air is very still in the summer, and it's always in the summer when my horses get sick. You can't train sick horses and you can't win races with horses that are not one hundred per cent fit, although we've only had a couple of bad years with sick horses and it happens everywhere, not just here.'

A more pressing dilemma is the number of horses in training at Barbury Castle and not their susceptibility to ill-health. At the start of the 1998 season Mikie had 36 horses in training but his landlord, Conrad Goess, has built another barn with room for an extra 17 horses, bringing capacity up to 51. Mikie pays Goess by the box, and it is written in his contract that by the year 2000 he must pay rent on all 51 boxes.

He says: 'If I am going to continue and make a success of this place I will have to get more horses in, which means finding new owners. I guess with everything that has happened in the last couple of years I've let things slip a bit. But I can't afford to rent empty boxes, that's for certain.'

'This might be a factor in my belief that it's time for a new challenge in my life, but I believe that one way God has of changing my course is to move my ambition maybe to do something else. I myself, like many other Christians, question it and say, "Why?"'

'Undoubtedly my illness has led to me seek God's will with a greater sense of urgency, but I am happy to just sit back and trust in Him. He hasn't let me down before. The fact that I am here training horses at Barbury Castle is a miracle in itself.

'It all came together, when the odds were at times stacked against it happening, because God was in it from the beginning. And He has kept me in a position as a trainer with enough horses to make the business go, so why has He allowed this to happen to me? It is very difficult to tell but when we look back, sometimes we can see why God has allowed things to happen.'

Mikie is convinced that God has brought and will continue to bring good out of the tragedy in his life. Tom McPherson and Mary O'Reilly felt the same way. They made sense of the disaster in their lives just as Mikie came to terms with his terrible injuries and illness, and other people's lives have been dramatically changed as a result of their faith in God. I know many people who were healed emotionally and physically by God after listening to the testimony of McPherson and O'Reilly, and Mikie is being used to reach people in much the same way.

His relationship with God is a dynamic force in his life. He lives for God, spending time in prayer before every decision, and his Bible is more indispensable each day than the *Racing Post*.

Despite his suffering Mikie has a great plan and a great vision for the future. Back in 1991 when he first came to Barbury Castle he wanted, more than anything else, to be a winner in his sport. Since the summer of 1992 when the fine bay filly called Massiba – which ironically is Arabic for disaster – came in first at Windsor races, Mikie has had over 100 winners and become something of a star in the world of horse racing. He mixes with the rich and famous and has the respect of some of the most powerful people in the business. Mikie's photo album is a Who's Who of royalty and celebrities – mention his name to the best trainers and jockeys in horse racing at the moment, or any legend of the sport, and watch their eyes light up.

Make no mistake, Mikie is a big man in horse racing. But the only thing he really cares about is creating a growing Christian presence in the sport. His burning desire is to see God's name glorified in horse racing, which sounds like a paradox, but in reality there is nothing absurd or unrealistic about it.

In March 1998 a delegation of members of the clergy, led by the Manchester United Football Club chaplain and director of SCORE (Soccer Chaplaincy Offering Resources and Encouragement) John Boyers, visited Barbury Castle Racing Stables to discuss an ambitious plan to look after the previously neglected spiritual needs of the horse-racing industry by introducing chaplains to racecourses up and down the country. All the top football clubs in Britain have a chaplain, and other sports are well represented by the clergy, but horse racing is something of a spiritual wilderness, with the exception of places like Newmarket where All Saints Church – the 'racing church' – performs an important role in the horse-racing community.

'There are a few Christians in the industry but by and large there is no real Christian presence in horse racing,' Mikie says. 'I don't know of many Christians in the sport, and I've been involved in the business for a long time and know a lot of people. It's an area that has been neglected for far too long, that's why I have prayed for a while for something to change.

'Chaplains involved in professional football, like John Boyers is at Manchester United, play a vital role in looking after the spiritual needs of that industry, but jockeys and trainers and all the other people involved in horse racing have nothing to fall back on when they have problems.'

It's true, jockeys have the same emotional and spiritual needs as footballers. They are faced with the same kind of problems, unique to professional sport: the constant pressure of being a winner and the agony of losing, and the mental and physical pain of always striving to stay on top. And in the case of jockeys, just staying alive.

When a jockey is seriously injured or killed, people involved in the sport inevitably question the fundamental reasons for pushing man and beast so hard, but then they accept it and deal with it and life goes on – except not everyone gets over it and a great emotional and spiritual healing is needed.

It's not just the extreme situation of serious injury or death that creates a need. There are huge financial pressures in horse racing that more often than not cause people to break down.

The signs are not always that obvious, but I have met trainers and jockeys in this country who admit they are crying out for someone to help ease their troubled hearts and minds.

One very rich owner, who has been involved in the sport for over thirty years, told me: 'There is a sickness in horse racing called greed, and it consumes people to the point of self-destruction. Many, many people at the top end of the sport need help because they can't cope with the pressures. At the races there are miles of smiles and popping corks and more money than the average working man will ever see, but behind the mask of this fragile world of gambling and social climbing is a world of empty, unfulfilled people whose only satisfaction is the sound of prize money being counted. I know because I'm one of them.'

The overall vision is to have a chaplain at every major training centre in Britain. 'It's an exciting thought,' Mikie says, 'because it will provide the whole industry with a spiritual foundation, and horse racing can only benefit from that. I have always prayed that we can help God to come into the racing industry.

'I have always had a thought in my mind, for years now, of setting up a prayer group to pray for the industry, for people involved with horse racing, and I have been quite annoyed with myself because I've been meaning to do something about it but haven't. I suppose I've been too demotivated to do it, for various reasons.

'And then a year or so ago I met this amazing Christian guy from America called Salty Roberts, who God has used in a big way to bring the Christian message to horse racing in the United States. Salty was a car park attendant at a track in America who could not read or write very well, but had a desire and a vision to evangelize horse racing in the USA. And through him there is now a chaplain at every track in America. He was led by God to bring the gospel message to the horse racing industry over here.'

John Boyers, one of the most influential chaplains in British sport, initially had his doubts about setting up a chaplaincy in horse racing, for reasons best known to himself, but in the time between Mikie's initial meeting with Salty Roberts and Boyer's visit to Barbury Castle, the director of SCORE had a change of heart, or more appropriately God changed it for him.

'Around September time 1997, after a lot of discussion and prayer, Salty linked up with a guy called Daryl Jackson, a Baptist Church evangelist, and shared with him our vision of setting up a chaplaincy in racing. Daryl then got in contact with John Boyers who said yes, it's a good idea.

'The timing was right, and God must have been in it because John said if anyone had asked him about setting up a chaplaincy in horse racing before he would have said no chance, but now it felt right. So he and Daryl and Salty had this meeting at Newmarket where Christians and non-Christians shared the vision for the future and Salty, because of his charismatic American religious culture, had everyone holding hands and praying.

'I think some people were a little upset because it was quite intense, perhaps embarrassing for some, especially those who were not particularly religious, but John came in and was able to settle the situation down. He said, "Look, our aim is not to evangelize horse racing or try and convert people in the industry to Christianity. The emphasis is pastoral care, we want to provide a caring and compassionate service that will meet the spiritual and emotional needs of all people involved in horse racing."

'He's a great guy, very down to earth and he knows what is needed. Salty is also a great guy and genuinely cares for the needs of people in horse racing, but people don't always respond to so-called "bible-bashing" and John's way is best. A chaplain's primary function is to be there for people in times of need, to listen and support and offer advice, just like the role of a vicar in the community.'

After hearing Mikie's vision for a chaplaincy in racing I talked to a dozen or so jockeys, trainers and race track staff at various courses in England and was amazed by the response. Almost everyone agreed it was a good idea and some of the stories I heard made me realize just what a tough sport it is, with many casualties of the intense pressure to win at all costs.

One top jockey, who asked to remain anonymous, admitted: 'A couple of years ago I hit a real bad patch where nothing was going right for me. I was injured most of the time and my form hit rock bottom. There was a lot of pressure on me to ride when I should have been resting, and at times I was taking my life in my hands because I was not focused and could not concentrate.

'My marriage was in trouble and I developed a real fear of getting seriously injured. One of my close friends died and I hit the bottle. I had no one to talk to and in the end I ended up going to a church in Ireland where my family live and just broke down crying. I'm not a religious man but the vicar of that church was a tower of strength, so I can see how having a chaplain at a track would help. I know many jockeys who would welcome the idea.'

The immediate plan is to install an experienced, ordained minister of some description as chaplain responsible for the pastoral care of the racing community at Newmarket, before the end of 1998. He will liaise with and be supported by All Saints Church and other local churches and will, in theory, spend two or three days each week in Newmarket where he will make himself available to jockeys, trainers, track officials, racecourse staff, in fact anyone involved in the sport.

'He will,' Mikie says, 'be caring for the entire horse-racing community at Newmarket, which is the biggest of its kind in Britain.

'The difference between here and America is that in the

States all racecourses are centres for a community. Horses are trained there, people live in villages built around the track and races take place most afternoons. It really is a thriving race track community, so setting up a Christian base headed by a chaplain was perhaps easier over there than it will be here.

'In England most of our tracks have no community around them. People just visit them on race day and go away again. We don't train horses at our race tracks and most of the time they are quite deserted. But Newmarket is a thriving community where thousands of different people mix seven days a week so it's the best place for us to start.

'Eventually we hope to have a chaplain at most of the racecourses in Britain, maybe part-time chaplains who spend half their time with local churches and the rest of the time providing pastoral care for the people involved at the track on race days. It will be a kind of network, so there will always be someone available for people to talk to.

'Primarily the chaplain will be ministering to people who are employed in the industry, but owners, who don't have as much contact with the day-to-day running of the sport, could also be reached. The bottom line is establishing God's presence in the sport, even on the gambling side of things because there is a lot of need there as well.'

Going back to Tom McPherson, who used to visit at least three different rodeos each week so he could deliver the gospel message to as many rodeo cowboys as possible, it is easier to preach to the unconverted when you have hard evidence of the existence or success of the thing that you want people to believe in.

Before he died McPherson told me: 'I guess it would have been harder for me to convince people of the existence and life-changing power of God had He not miraculously healed me. I can imagine what some folks would have said to me had I wheeled into a rodeo and started preaching to them from my wheelchair. I can hear them now: "Why hell Tom, God certainly ain't done much to help you, has he now?"

McPherson had a point and Mikie admits: 'I guess some people look at me and think, "How can he talk about the love of God – poor guy, his faith in God hasn't helped him at all!"

'In fact one of my owners, after finding out about my illness, said, "Hey Mikie, you must have done something really bad in your previous life to deserve this." It was a tongue-in-cheek remark but there is a serious side to it. People could find it hard to believe what I have to say because of what has happened to me, and I suspect many people whisper behind my back saying, "How can he believe in God after all that's happened to him?" It's inevitable really. We all ask, "Why?"'

In a sport where people sell their souls for a chance to strike it lucky amid the mad rush of thundering hooves and silk-clad riders wielding whips to chase vanishing dreams and pots of gold, Michael Heaton-Ellis is something of an outsider. He believes the only dead certainty in this life is God's promise of eternal life, although in his weaker moments, when the dark thoughts threaten to destroy his peace, Michael finds it hard to imagine life after death.

There is a verse of scripture in the New Testament that Mikie and I have often discussed, 1 Corinthians 13, verse 12: 'For now we see through a glass, darkly; but then face to face: Now I know in part; but then shall I know even as also I am known.'

This is not a cryptic message. It is plain truth. There are secret things that are hidden from the world that only God knows, and none of them will be revealed until we get to Heaven. One day Mikie will know the real reason, but maybe accepting this verse of scripture is the only way to end the soul-destroying struggle to answer the big question: Why?

10
....

The Truth Will Always Be

For a man in a wheelchair Michael Heaton-Ellis has done an awful lot of running. Excuse the pun, but his feet never touched the ground after he left hospital following the terrible accident that almost killed him nearly twenty years ago, and for the best part of a decade he was a man on a mission; hell bent on proving to the whole world that nothing could stop him from doing what he wanted to do.

His body had been weakened but his mind was strong, and right in the middle of that God-shaped hole in his soul Michael Heaton-Ellis had crammed a skyscraper of ambition. It reached up into the stars of his gaping dreams and climbed high over his future. He could reach anything from here and all the world scurried beneath like ants to his towering hope.

There is a theory that each and every one of us has a God-shaped hole in our soul. I call it a theory because belief, no matter how strong, should not be rammed home like a fistful of pills down the throat of humanity, no matter how sick it gets. So, whether you accept it or not, this theory has its place in the collective voice of the free world because of free speech and free will and the equal rights of both the freethinker and dogmatist.

This is Mikie's theory and the theory of many, many other 'believers'. The God-shaped hole is a missing piece of jigsaw:

the jigsaw of life, and nothing else in the entire universe can fit into this hole. God is the key to completing the jigsaw of life and only when this final piece is in place can a person be complete.

But it doesn't stop people from trying to fill the hole with all kinds of different shapes and sizes of jigsaw pieces. Michael Heaton-Ellis crammed in a skyscraper of ambition, but you can use almost anything to try to fill the gap. Ambition is a popular choice because it's got a nice feel to it and is extremely pliable; it can be moulded into any form – achievement, money, power, success – but sometimes it's simpler to use ready-made pieces that are easier to come by like drugs, sex, violence – and religion.

Some may wake up one morning and say, 'God, my life is so boring and unfulfilling,' and go and climb a mountain or change their job or their partner or just stay in bed and feel sorry for themselves. But none of these things fills the hole in a person's soul. It can be real fun trying, because some of the things we do in search of fulfilment and peace of mind are very rewarding and make us feel good, while some things leave us feeling empty and hurt. It's a lottery where the only winners are those who have faith and peace in God.

If Michael Heaton-Ellis never trains another successful racehorse, he's still a winner. That is because in the biggest race of all, he has followed the winning strategy. I'm not talking about training a Derby winner or having a runner come home first in the Grand National. The biggest race of all is from the cradle to the grave and beyond; beyond God's winning post.

Mikie is not a superman but there are times when he tried to be. He powered his steel wheelchair with an iron will; the terrible accident that destroyed his life did not shatter his strong heart and determination. Set it back, perhaps, as he rehabilitated for a year, but did not shatter it. The seeming unfairness of losing a potential riding career was nothing compared to the joy of being alive, and Mikie remembers being totally confident that God would heal him, even though he didn't have faith in God.

After all, everything else had gone right in his life before the accident. He had achieved what he set out to do, and walking again was just another challenge. It angered him that the doctors gave him no hope at all. He did not believe them when they told him that his injuries were permanent. He was in control of his life. He always had been. This was merely a temporary setback. There were no tears, no remorse, no self-pity.

To strive means to try hard. Mikie tried very hard to put the pieces of his life back together and succeeded. We all strive and many reach their ultimate goal, some against incredible odds and in the face of terrible suffering, because the human spirit is remarkably tough. But sometimes our best shot is not enough and we can end up empty-handed, unfulfilled and maybe even dead.

The death of young jockey Richard Davis in a steeple-chasing fall in July 1996 stunned the racing world, but even more sobering is what Davis told a journalist friend of mine six months before his life so tragically ended at the age of 26. 'I'm feeling a little tired today,' he said. 'Always striving for that big win, always striving to find enough rides to make a living. But you've got to keep going, got to keep believing, even when you know it could all come crashing down around your ears.'

Davis was an ordinary jockey. A journeyman jump jockey of some promise, but just one of the many who flog around the country every season trying to make an honest wage from a dangerous game. He was riding a useless horse named Mr Sox in a novices' handicap chase at Southwell, Nottinghamshire, on 19 July 1996. Mr Sox slammed into the first fence at around 30 miles per hour, catapulting Davies over his head.

A split second after the jockey hit the ground Mr Sox landed on top of him.

In the jargon of jump jockeys Davis was 'buried' by his horse. He was pronounced dead three hours and twenty minutes later. The extent of the damage to his crushed internal organs was horrific. His inferior vena cava – the main vein of the body which leads into the heart – had been torn three-quarters of the way across, flooding his abdomen with five pints of blood, and his liver had been split. The official cause of death was a lacerated liver combined with internal bleeding.

At Davis's funeral Richard Dunwoody, three times champion and arguably the finest rider of his generation, recited the words of the Saw Doctors song 'To Win Just Once', that has become something of an anthem for the jump jockeys. The chorus goes: 'To win just once, that would be enough,' but it rarely ever is. It's human nature to resist the urge to quit, especially when one is striving to be the best.

In 1990 I met Jonjo O'Neill, that great scrapper of a man whose life as a jockey and trainer has been overloaded with a sickening amount of crisis. I'd read somewhere O'Neill quoted as saying, 'Will power is stronger than any religion,' but a friend of his told me, 'That's not the Jonjo I know. He's a God-fearing man who prays.' I was writing a newspaper article about how people fight cancer in different ways.

Cancer that looked like being terminal, terrible injuries, the threatened amputation of a leg and the devastation of his marriage rattled O'Neill's life like a storm shaking a tree. But, as Hugh McIlvanney wrote in the *Observer* on 11 March 1990, 'Whatever power allocates the tough times in life should have learned by now that there is no point in trying to break Jonjo O'Neill. He is not the cracking kind.'

O'Neill actually told McIlvanney: 'You should have some strength to spare after coming through that lot. In my own life, I feel nobody ever had a better education in how to cope with the disappointments and frustrations of a trainer's existence. Bearing grudges or feeling sorry for yourself does no one any good. You've got to kick into the rest of your life.'

Mikie had a similar philosophy before he committed his life to God, especially identifying with O'Neill's analogy that 'a marriage break-up is a bit like having a serious fall as a rider – once the bruising comes out it's not so bad.'

But there is another side to O'Neill; a strand of this wiry Irishman that proved to me that even the 'not for cracking kind' need God. 'I'm not a religious man,' he said, 'but yes, it's true I have prayed for help and strength. None of us is big enough or tough enough to say we don't need it from time to time.'

A few years ago, during a trip to America, I met a guy called Bob Wieland who had both his legs blown off by a Vietnamese land mine in 1969. To some people he was a freak, and I admit that the first time I saw him walking on his hands with his torso swinging to and fro I was shocked. When they found what was left of Bob after the mine went off underneath him, his army buddies said, 'Jesus, I hope he's dead.'

It was not a pretty sight, but not half as bad as what they imagined Bob's life would be like if he survived. And yet Bob's desire to live was so strong that he never doubted for a moment that he could carry on without his legs, even though he had been a brilliant athlete before the accident and had been looking forward to a professional career in baseball once the war in Vietnam was over.

So Bob started living life to the full and striving to be someone. He pushed himself to the limit and pulled off crazy stunts like completing a three-year walk on his hands across America, the New York and Los Angeles marathons and the

Hawaii Ironman Triathlon. But the day I met Bob he admitted: 'Only a fool would do all these things and believe they can fill the God-shaped hole in their life. To most people, it looks as though I am doing it all – "What a hero, what courage," they say, but what they don't know is that I'm not doing very much at all. It's one hundred per cent God, zero per cent Bob.

'God has a purpose in putting me in all these situations, so that I can demonstrate to people who perhaps don't have the measure of faith that God is the one who dwells in me. He is the same God who can dwell in them. I realized that day in Vietnam that I was going to have to totally rely on God. I was physically as weak as a baby. And so, at that time, I began praying that God would give me a dose of his weakness, and every day it's the same. The weakness of God is stronger than any man's strength.'

The only real difference between Bob Wieland's testimony and Mikie's story is the timing of their realization that they were going to have to totally rely on God. For a long time after his accident Mikie relied on his own strength, and it wasn't until after years of trying to fill the God-shaped hole in his life with piece after piece of his own burning ambition and striving that he eventually found what he was looking for: Jesus.

Before Mikie powered his wheelchair across the finish line of the 1989 London Marathon in less than three hours to raise over £50,000 for charity, he had already made a success of his life by defying the odds to pursue his dream of training racehorses, and at the same time become a key figure in the horse-racing industry. But he was still empty inside and suddenly realized that he had got it all wrong. The hole in the jigsaw of his life was caused by alienation from God and not any emotional, mental or physical deficiency in his life. What he needed was spiritual fulfilment; the only way to become a complete person.

Mikie had been angry at God since the accident, but now he saw that God was angry at him. He had been the centre of his world – a rich, colourful world of horses, and money, and beautiful women all woven like golden strands into the rich tapestry of racing – and treated God as he had treated other people in his life, as servants or stepping stones to get what he wanted and where he wanted. Now he saw that life was really about serving God. He had got it all upside down. That great skyscraper of ambition in his life was not so much a stairway to heaven as a helter-skelter to hell.

Ralph Crathorne, an old friend, explained that God loved Mikie, that He had sent His Son Jesus to end the awful alienation by dying for Mikie on a cross. He could be God's friend, God would never desert him or let him down like luck and his wife and other people had already done. Furthermore Jesus had risen from the dead. He was alive today, and He longed for Mikie to commit his life to Him.

The next day Mikie met the vicar who had married Katie O'Sullivan and him a few years earlier. The vicar explained what was now clear to Mikie as the 'way of salvation'. The steps he should take were: Admit that he was a sinner and needed God; believe that Jesus, the Son of God, had died on the Cross so he could be forgiven; count the cost of following Jesus – He must be in control from then on; decide by an act of will to follow Jesus.

Later that night Mikie looked through the Bible references Ralph Crathorne and the vicar had given him and prayed that Jesus would take over his life. Initially he felt very little and prayed that prayer of commitment repeatedly over the next few days in order to make sure it was real.

There were many things he was unsure about and his understanding was far from complete, but there was no need to worry because in heaven, where angels sing for joy every time a soul is saved, Jesus had already added Mikie's name to the book of eternal life. God had seen inside the heart of a man who was truly sorry for leaving Him out for so long, and inside the father heart of God there was great happiness.

Mikie learned how to read the Bible in such a way that he could apply it to his life day by day. He learned how to pray, and how to talk about his faith. For the first time in his life he began to see true direction and he had a great sense of peace. His striving was over because he had reached God's winning post. The missing piece of the jigsaw was in place.

From this moment on Michael Heaton-Ellis stopped running. Deep in his soul he knew that with God on his side he could cope with anything.